AS FOR ME AND MY HOUSE:

Some Redemptive Words for The Black Family

AS FOR ME AND MY HOUSE:
Some Redemptive Words
for
The Black Family

By

Alvin C. Bernstine

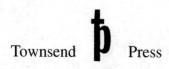

Townsend ‡ Press

Nashville, Tennessee
1993

Dedicated to My House

Kamira Damali, Akinlawon Camau, Kamilah Diarri;

MY QUEEN

Karen Denise Jones-Bernstine

Table of Contents

Foreword

Much has been written in recent years about the crises and challenges facing the Black/African American Family in modern society. Such challenges as rising crime rates, increased use of drugs and alcohol, violence, illiteracy, illegitimacy, and the heedless abandonment of the traditional values that once undergirded family life are described in numerous treatises with solid supporting statistics, but seldom are found methods of attack and practical solutions for these problems. Therein lies a major reason why I am so pleased to be asked to write the Foreword for **As For Me and My House; Some Redemptive Words for the Black Family,** a collection of sermons devoted to Family Ministry by the Reverend Alvin Bernstine. Not only does Rev. Bernstine enumerate and describe the grave problems facing Black families today; he also helps the Black Family recognize, analyze and combat many of the major problems currently experienced by lifting up the role of the Black church in modern life, and providing spiritual insights and illumination available to the Black Family from within this perspective.

Reverend Bernstine's pastoral experience and position as Director of Family Ministry at the Sunday School Publishing Board have well qualified him to prepare the sermons which constitute this seminal statement on The Black Family. I foresee great use of this document as a text in courses on Family Ministry; and as a "how-to" book on approaching societal problems within the family through the church; and as a basis for sermon-building.

Cecelia N. Adkins

Executive Director
Sunday School Publishing Board
National Baptist Convention, U.S.A.,
Incorporated

PREFACE

Recent years have generated a growing concern for the Black/African American family. Experts and non-experts, informed by a diversity of disciplines and opinions, have expressed their many views concerning the crises and challenges of the Black family. Interestingly, the Black family has historically been interesting fodder for fledgling academicians and social scientists. However, this current wave of variegated views and opinions does not exclusively represent those with academic interest. Many of the current voices represent the people of the African American family, who are not merely pursuing academic goals. Presently, there is an ever growing catina of those who have lived and breathed the phenomenal life of the families of ex-slaves and they have begun contributing greatly to the on-going discussion. It appears that we are taking seriously the often mentioned belief that no one can help us better than ourselves.

The writer of this work joins in with the chorus of those bred, born, and nurtured within the experience of the Black family. The following thoughts are not offered for academic objectives, although academia contributes to their formulation. I present these thoughts as one who is greatly concerned about the health and hope of the Black family. The voice that I add to the concerned voices for the Black family comes from a constant presence in the Black community—the Black church.

The Black church remains a powerful force in the shaping of the African American community. The Black church has provided me the platform and perspective from which to approach the continuing challenges of the African American family. From the pulpit of the Black church I have struggled to offer a word of hope and promise, for those of us who know the struggles of being the Black family in White America. The following pages represent some sermonic perspectives that have been offered from the pathos of "me and my house."

The messages have, for the most part, maintained their speaking form and language. They have, however, been categorized to coincide with particular dimensions of Black family life. For instance, messages for the general family, messages for the Black father, messages for the Black mother, messages on Black children, single-parenting, etc. I am pleased to have the following poetic contributions from my mother and daughter.

A MOTHER'S DAY TRIBUTE
In Loving Memory of Our Mother
(and our Grandmother)
MATTIE BOLEN - MILES
A Beautiful Garden

We keep in our hearts a picture to be remembered
Of the sacrifices you so unselfishly rendered.
You left with us an eternal guiding light
In patience, courage and the will to fight.
For the love of God and services to your Church
Was a reason for living and giving so much.
Let us all be swift to hear and see
The results of hope, faith, prayer and sincerity.
Although you were plucked from this room,
The memory of your life is like a flower in bloom.

Maxine Miles - Highsmith

MOTHER

Mother dear, she is mine,
Offers her services all the time.
Thankful to God for her every day,
Humble, gently, she leads the way.
Enduring and sweetness she displays,
Remembering her strength and
courage always.

Maxine Miles - Highsmith

MOTHERS ARE SPECIAL

*Written by Kamira Damali Bernstine as
a First Grader*

Mothers are so special,
You can see they help
you do so many things
that you start doing them yourself.

Mothers are so special
when they help you get dressed.
They help you undress, too.

Mothers are very special.
I like when you take us to Krogers,
where we can get on the horse ride.
I like when we were at swimming class,
when I jumped from the diving board.

I like when you take us to the park
and let us ride our bikes.
I like to have surprise parties,
and birthday parties.

Thank you for doing all those things for me.
I love all those things. I love you!
Mothers are so special.

A BEAUTIFUL VISION

HURT NO LIVING THING.
NOT HUNGRY BIRD NOR PESTY FLY;
NOT HARMLESS ANT NOR LADY BUG;
NOT BUTTERFLY NOR DRAGON FLY;
NOT BEETLE NOR DRAGON FLY;
NOR CATERPILLAR.
THEY ARE SO HARMLESS.
LET'S NOT KILL INSECTS,
OR ANY HARMLESS LIVING THING.

Kamira Damali Bernstine
"A Princess With A Beautiful Vision"

AS FOR ME AND MY HOUSE:
A Family Resolve With Faithful Results

Text: *"Now therefore fear the Lord, and serve him in sincerity and in faithfulness; put away the gods which your fathers served beyond the River, and in Egypt, and serve the Lord. And if you be unwilling to serve the Lord, choose this day whom you will serve, whether the gods your fathers served in the region beyond the River, or the gods of the Amorites in whose land you dwell; but as for me and my house, we will serve the Lord."*
Joshua 24:14-15 (RSV)

I do not know how true the tale is, but legend speaks of a famous feud between the Hatfields and the McCoys. Movies have been created that dramatized the intergenerational battle between these two families. It appeared that a Hatfield lived to do battle with a McCoy, and a McCoy lived to do battle with a Hatfield. The purpose for which the particular members of these two families lived was to do one another in. Children were bred and born to do battle with Hatfields or McCoys. Just think about it! You come into the world and your every day has been shaped to do battle with a Hatfield or a McCoy. The truth is: we usually rise no higher than the aspirations of our families. Whatever vision dominates one's family has tremendous influence upon the individuals of the family.

I am aware of the many exceptions, but the dominant trend suggests that we rise no higher than the prevailing aspirations of our families. The family that immerses itself in lofty goals and noble achievements generally arranges life so that the aspired goals of the family are eventually achieved through its members. On the other hand, the family that saturates itself in a lot of trashy ideas and slick schemes to go nowhere fast usually produces a multitude of social deviants, who plague the society with trifling and ignoble deeds. Moreover, the bottom line of a family's aspirations is determined by whom the family serves.

Joshua seemed to have understood the decisive power of a family's god. In a daring adventure on Shechem, Joshua called the people together to consider their relationship with God. God had liberated the people from the oppressive servitude of having to "make bricks without straw." God covenanted with the people through the mountainous rendezvous with Moses, God's servant. The trials of the wilderness had deepened their understanding of the holiness of God. Since Joshua's rise to leadership, God had blessed them with precious portions of the Promised Land. For a brief period of progress and profit, the former slaves of Egypt basked in the prosperity of God's promise.

How unpopular Joshua must have appeared, as he interrupted the prosperity march of the people. I can only imagine what the initial response could have been, when this old preacher staggered out of the woodwork and summoned that upbeat crowd to a business meeting on Shechem. Joshua, well advanced in years, had apparently remained an influential presence in the life of the people, for when he called for the meeting, no excuses were offered. The people quickly made their way to the meeting, so that they could hear his words. Joshua reminded the people how faithful God had been, and then called attention to the people's need to renew their relationship with God. Joshua understood that further blessings from God depended upon their faithfulness to God. The upward reaches of the people would be determined by their willingness to serve God wholeheartedly.

Joshua said, "You choose...but as for me and my house, we will serve the Lord." Joshua's proposal is as relevant today as it was then. Serving the God of our liberation assures our families of some faithful results. Serving God leads to the development of the best within us. Our potential to soar high, dream lofty, reach up, and travel far is tied to our willingness to serve God. The results of our journey will be dependent upon our families' resolve to risk all for God. Our families, when anchored by a determination to serve God, unleash tremendous possibilities for human accomplishment. In simpler terms, we soar no higher than the God we serve.

What makes a message like this so important today is because there are absolutely too many of our people content with low aspirations. A dangerous number of our people are satisfied with doing as little as possible, with themselves. We have become satisfied with no ideas, small ambitions, no goals, petty possibilities, and empty dreams. Too many of the people coming out of our families have no get-up about going anywhere, because they are happy at being nowhere. The gods that are being served in our families have set some scary limits on where we are going as a people.

Joshua mentions two objects of service that limit the aspirations of God's people. We don't like for people to expose our loyalties, especially if they explain why we are no better than we are. Joshua understood the nature of prophetic leadership which calls people to the best within them, even if it means exposing the worst about them. Joshua saw people clinging on to the gods of their past bondage, as well as accumulating some contemporary gods for a new bondage.

My mystic mentor, Thomas Merton, noted that the devil believes in God; he just doesn't serve God. Joshua saw evidence of people serving the gods of their past bondage. Some latter day Joshua needs to call us to Shechem and alert us to our tendencies to serve the gods of our past bondages. He/she would have ample evidence because so many of us are really no better off than when we were unsaved. God has been ever so kind to us, delivered us from so many

Egypts. God has brought us through wildernesses, brought down walls, carried us over Jordans; but we are reaching no higher than we were back then.

The gods of our pre-salvation still have a hold on us. We are serving them, and trying to fool God. So many of us cannot cut loose the gods that dragged us to the ground; as a result, we are setting up other family members to repeat our failures. Being saved ought to have some positive effects on our lives. We may cannot claim perfection (and none of us can), but we ought to be looking a little better, acting a little better, being a little better than we were before we met Jesus.

Joshua saw how some of the people had been freed of the influence of their past gods. He saw that some people had distanced themselves from the gods of their past. However, he saw that some new gods had taken the old gods' place. Jesus mentioned something about a house being emptied of demons, yet was taken over by seven more. The result was that the house once possessed by one had become seven-times more dangerous. Substituting one devil for another does not make one devil-free.

A lot of us may be doing better on one hand. On the other hand, we are much worse off. Our house may be bigger, but our home no happier. We may have more entertainment centers, but less communication center. We may have more cars to individually drive, but fewer places to go as a family. We may have more money in the bank, but spend less time with the children. We may have more education, but less knowledge of Jesus Christ. The land of the Americans is as seductive as the land of the Amorites.

The Amorites, like America, were a strong nation, with wealth and power, as well as culture and learning. All nations looked toward the Amorites. America has a whole lot going for it. People of other countries respect America. All nations, friend or foe, look toward America. However, there are some gods in America that have sucked in a lot of us. A lot of our families have begun to serve the gods of America. The gods of America are selfishness, rather than community. The gods of America are greed, rather than generosity. The gods of America are getting over, rather than getting along. The gods of America are sexism and racism. The gods of America will have us stepping on people that we should be helping. A lot of us are within families that serve the gods of the Americas, in the land in which we now dwell.

Many so-called smart Blacks rarely attend church. The Black church has become primitive and overly emotional for many. We promote a "go-when-you- feel-like-it" approach to church. A whole lot of folk have literally dumped the church. Too many of us are well in certain areas, but terribly sick in others. We now serve the gods of the Americas—greed, individualism, oppression, sexism, and racism.

Joshua summoned the people to the mountain to consider their relationship with God. He saw the possibilities for families to either live or die, fly high or sink low, go far or fall short. He understood that a family reaches no higher than the gods they serve. Once he laid out the choices, he stated the resolve of his family. "As for me and my house, we will serve the Lord."

What are some of the possibilities provided when families resolve to serve God? Joshua helps us to see that a family resolved to serve God, first of all, develops initiative. Joshua announced the decision of his family. His family had made a conscious choice to serve God. Whenever we make the choice to serve God, God honors us for taking redemptive initiative. God made us as creatures with wills. We have the power to choose, to determine our directions and aspirations. We determine how high our families will reach, by the choices of the god we will serve.

Choosing God develops initiative, over against falling into the seductive choices of our world. I know too many families that are just going along. Whichever way the winds of society blow, that's where many of our families will be. We are so into trying to keep up, or stay behind. Yes, there are some of us who do all we can to stay behind. We are committed to not raising up any higher than our parents. We don't want to see ourselves doing better than they. As a result, we arrange family life so that very few surpass the accomplishments of the former generation.

Our families need to be gripped by initiative. Active choices must be made to give God your best. Someone has said, "What I am is God's gift to me. What I make of myself is my gift to God." The same can be said of our families. Our families must make the choice to give God their best.

Joshua helps us to see that a family resolved to serve God, secondly, develops identity. Joshua emphasizes the pronouns of personal identity, "As for me and my house, we will serve the Lord." A resolve to serve the Lord props us up where we desperately need to be propped up. A sense of identity could be a marvelous thing for our families. Our children could be saved a lot of pain, in their search for self, if families knew who they were. I shall always cherish Alex Haley's Roots, for directing my search for self. Roots brought me back home, to my family, where I most needed to be.

The heathenistic practices of many of our families does serious damage to children's sense of identity. A child who does not know who he/she is will do most anything. In Kunjufu's "Up Against The Wall", young Shawn is able to overcome the walls once he has courageously affirmed who he is. He was able to dodge many destructive practices by holding to what he believed most about himself, that had been taught in the family.

A child who knows who he is, is less likely to murder, for murder is essentially self-destruction. Our children need the strength of esteem that comes most powerfully from knowing who you are. "As for me and my house...."

Finally, Joshua helps us to see that a family resolved to serve God develops inner strength. The Bible says, "The people served God all the days of Joshua...." The resolution of Joshua provided the moral fortitude necessary to ward off tough times. Gods of our past, and the gods of America, they only rob us of strength. Idol gods never give, they only take away. But the God, who brought us out of the places of our bondages, He giveth strength in times of weakness.

Our families need inner strength to be able to stand during the difficult moments. Inner strength would enable our families to stick together, when Satan lashes out with all of his vicious fury, ...with all of his deceitful plots, ...with all of his unholy methods, ...with all of his destructive forces, ...with all of his despicable ingenuity, ...with all of his hateful and harmful tactics.

My youngest daughter gave an animated rendition of the "Itsy-Bitsy Spider." In her special tones she sang, "Itsy-Bitsy Spider, went up the water spout. And down came the rain and washed the spider out. Out came the sun and dried up the rain, and the itsy-bitsy spider came out once again."

Brothers and Sisters, in every family some rain shall fall. In every family, a washout will come. In every family, some pain will visit. In every family, dark nights shall come. But when the "Son" comes to see about you, rains dry out. The washouts pass over. The pain stops. The nights turn into mornings, and by our inner strength—WE CAN ALL COME OUT AGAIN!

A VIEW OF THE FAMILY FROM
THE PIGPEN

Text: *"Then He said: "A certain man had two sons. And the younger of them said to his father, 'Father, give me the portion of goods that falls to me.' So he divided to them his livelihood. And not many days after, the younger son gathered all together, journeyed to a far country, and there wasted his possessions with prodigal living. But when he spent all, there arose a severe famine in that land, and he began to be in want. Then he went and joined himself to a citizen of that country, and he sent him into his fields to feed swine. And he would gladly have filled his stomach with the pods that the swine ate, and no one gave him anything. But when he came to himself, he said, 'How many of my father's hired servants have bread enough and to spare, and I perish with hunger! I will arise and go to my father, and will say to him, "Father, I have sinned against heaven and before you, and I am no longer worthy to be called your son. Make me like one of your hired servants." And he arose and came to his father. But when he was still a great way off, his father saw him and had compassion, and ran and fell on his neck and kissed him."* (**Luke 15:11-20**, New King James Version)

I have been in a lot of fruitless conversations and discussions. I have painfully endured discussions that led to nowhere. In retrospect, the reason so many conversations and discussions produce no helpful results is because so often the discussions themselves miss the point. We can talk ever so eloquently, argue passionately, even get a few folk on our side; but if we miss the point, nothing will be resolved. This is often the sad state of political discussions. Unfortunately, a lot of family and church discussions veer far from the mark.

I can think of one growing phenomenon in our country, where everybody seems to miss the point. I speak of homelessness, where growing numbers of people are fending for themselves outside of socially expected norms. In New York City, Ph.D's are living in cardboard condominiums, stacked neatly next to one another, with welcome mats placed outside of makeshift doors. In Berkeley, California, the city has surrendered one of its major parks to roving vagabonds, who push shopping carts carrying all of their earthly possessions. People's Park has become a kind of hobo country club, housing entire families under makeshift tents and plywood covers. Nashville has over a thousand people living on the streets, erecting tents next to freeways, living in abandoned cars, and developing a riverside neighborhood. At the banks of the river, there lives a legless man in an old abandoned car. He performs all of the functions of nature within hobbling range of his rusted out domain.

Thousands of children have been born on the streets, and the only life they know is bumming and beggary. Many have never slept on a mattress, never seen a dishwasher, and the closest thing to a bathroom has been public facilities. We live in the richest country in the world, where five-thousand dollar dinners are held to fatten campaign purses and children live who have never sat in a bathtub. The real problem with all of this is that those who speak of helping the homeless are largely missing the point.

We are daily confronted with down-and-out people, standing at freeway exits, with signs saying "Homeless! Will work for food...." It is most unfortunate that the very people being subjected to this massive "hobo" lifestyle have joined in the discussion that really misses the point. I say that the point is being missed because much of the discussion centers around jobs, poverty, and economic depression. The basic issue that needs to be discussed has nothing to do with not having a house; a foreclosed mortgage; or a job shipped overseas. The issue that needs to be discussed is helping people to live in relationships, something that Jesus talked about so long ago.

Most of the people living on the streets of our cities are persons who have had relationships destroyed. Homelessness is not houselessness, nor joblessness. It is living outside of functional relationships. I don't believe anyone here can lose a job, lose a house, fall on bad times, and have nowhere to lay their heads. I can fall on the worst of times, and some family member will at least give me a mat on the floor, a cot in some room, a hideaway bed under some roof. There is no such thing as falling on such devastating economic difficulties that your family turns its back on you. However, we can destroy relationships so that no one in our families will want anything to do with us.

The story of the prodigal son addresses the consequences of what can happen to all who break relationship with their family. It is the story of a family suffering from the choices made by individual members. The choice of the younger son was to separate himself and all that he had inherited from the influences of his family. He no longer wanted to be constrained by the values, ideals, and ethics of his family. He wanted out! He wanted to put distance between himself and the moral balances that held in check his wild and youthful urges. He wanted nothing else to do with the "thou shalts" and "thou shalt nots" that are built into healthy family life. The stuff of family living was no longer important to him. He wanted to do his own thing, without some family member looking over his shoulder and questioning whether he was right or wrong.

There is a lot of talk going on about dysfunctional families. We even made up a word to define our inability to accept and understand the uniqueness of each family unit. I am not convinced that families have become totally dysfunctional. All families are functioning, they just may not be able to do all things well. If we began labeling families dysfunctional, then we better all jump into the boat of dysfunctionality, because no family is doing all things well.

It is impossible to do all things well within a family. We all became family out of something that has been stamped within our soul called divine intention. God put something within us that can never be erased that forces family out of us, even when we don't want it. It is called "it's not good for human beings to live alone."

God's intention for us to live in relationship drives us into family situations, even when we do not care to be in family. We are stuck in family. We are family for life. Relationships are eternal, even if we find ourselves in homeless communes living in cardboard condominiums. Homeless people have ironically come together as the community of broken relationships.

The younger son, like so many of us, thought he would be an exception. He thought he was slicker than everybody else who tried to live outside of family. He asked the father to give him his portion. "Give me what I've got coming. I am tired of these old, out-dated family rules. I want to try something different, free of all of this parental restraint and homey hogwash."

It is most interesting that he could not even leave home without taking home with him. He had to get something from home, before he could leave home. He is very slick, but so much like many of us. He thought he could take the best that home offered and make it away from home. The story is that he went on out there. He went far away from the restraints and controls of family influence. He did what he could not help but do. He wasted himself. He lived wildly, free of controls, free of checks and balances. He did his thing and came up empty. He let it all hang out and ended up with nothing. He tried to have a good time off all the stuff of his family, away from his family, and came up on the short end.

Jesus put it like this, "After he had spent everything, a severe famine hit the whole country." I believe it's Brook

Benton who sings the song, "A Rainy Night In Georgia." Benton says that the rain is so severe in Georgia that it seems like it's raining all over the world. One night Arsenio Hall joked about the song, wondering what could have made the man think that Georgia was the whole world. Arsenio must not know that when difficulties come into one's life, it makes the whole world look difficult. When a heart is broken, the whole world breaks up. The world can only be understood from our corner in the world. Wherever we stand, sit, or lie, our eyes fall upon our world.

The famine of the younger son made it seem like it was famine all over the world. The want of his soul created a deep want in his world. When the young man found himself in an existential depression, the entire country fell in depression. What a lesson for America, even Black America, the depression of our economy reflects the depression of our relationships. We are as far away from healthy economics, as we are from healthy family life. Like the young man, "It is raining in our families, and it seems like it's raining all over the world."

An emptiness seized the young man. The friends he thought he had were fair weather friends. They left as soon as his substance left. When he went broke, they split the scene. Jesus tells us that the young man fell far from the values and teachings of his family. He hired himself out to those his family had taught him to avoid. He took employment from the citizenry of the far country. The Bible describes his employment as a feeder of pigs. Jews would never touch pigs, let alone feed pigs. Pigs are considered unholy by Jewish people. Yet, how many unholy things we find ourselves doing when away from the influence of family. Away from the moral strength of our family, we are subject to do anything. He spent time in the pig-pen. He became a servant of the most despicable elements of his culture. He sunk into the lowest depths.

It has become too common now for parents to lead children into crime. I have spiritually cringed at the all too frequent accounts of children assisting parents in drug traffic. Mothers and fathers, of ebony hue, have sunk so low that they think nothing of turning their own children out. From my little seat in the universe, it looks like whole families have sunk into the pigpen. No family will survive on the empty husks of drug traffic. You might make it for a few days, but in the end you will come up empty. We can accumulate all the money we can, but if our families lack the substances of love, grace, and community, we come up empty.

The younger son helps us to see something of powerful significance. In these days of family disdain, an ancient Bible character helps us to see that an appreciable perspective of the family is most often viewed when we are farthest from it. In this age of everyone-for-him/herself, an empty stomach Bible boy helps us to see that the farther we are away from family, the more we learn to appreciate it. In a society that has put everything up for grabs, including family values, a hungry eyed Bible boy helps us to see more profoundly: the only time we really gain something is when we lose it. From the pig-pen, the prodigal helps us to see that a sense of family can be mentally stabilizing. With pig feces oozing up through the holey soles of his shoes, a broken, homeless Bible boy comes to his senses as to the value of family.

We should value our families because they have the powerful potential of stabilizing our wandering minds. It does not matter how crazy a family may be (and surely whole families can be crazy), a sense of home can be a sobering source of strength. The young man came to his senses and his senses were directed to his family. Our families provide an anchoring for us that does not allow us to drift too far. It is no secret that the most fatal of all mental diseases is when one's mind just drifts. A lot of mental illness accompanies homeless people. Schizophrenia, neuroses, and all kinds of depressions have countless people just drifting. When one's mind leaves home, the consequences are most tragic.

I have a sister who once took leave from all sense of family. She drifted from job-to-job, many of them well paying. She allowed a two-hundred and fifty thousand dollar home to be unnecessarily foreclosed. Her youngest daughter, now nineteen, virtually had no mother for about ten years. My sister left the anchoring influence of her family upbringing. How often do we hear parents bemoaning their children's flight by noting, "They sure was not brought up that way." I shared with you on yesterday, that the intrigue of <u>Roots</u> led me back to the stabilizing influence of family.

There is an interesting account of an encounter Jesus had with a man. The man had broken all ties with family and society. He was considered homeless, although he made the town cemetery his residence. He was totally out of control. A whole lot of things were wrong with the man. Jesus came along and rescued the man from the many demons that tormented the man, keeping him out of healthy relationships. The healing of this tormented man is uniquely described as his being placed in his right mind. Of great interest to us is that when the man went to follow Jesus, Jesus told the man to go home. The man was trying to leave home. He wanted to go with Jesus, who was also being kicked out of His community. But Jesus told the man to go home.

Our families can be accurate registers for our mental health. If we can make it in our homes, we can make it anywhere. From the pigpen, a young man helps us to catch a view of the mental stability of family. Our family can reach us, even in a pigpen. The values, dreams, and hopes

15

of our family will come and shake us and place us in our right mind. Our senses can be recovered from the mental craziness of pigpen living, by a redemptive glimpse of family living. "I can help myself, as well as my family, if I get up out of this pigpen."

Dr. Samuel D. Proctor, my current preaching mentor, mused with us over the unspoken power of the Prodigal's mother. No mother is mentioned in the story, but we all know no father has children without a mother. Dr. Proctor imaginatively suggested that the most powerful influence of this pigpen bound boy may well have been the boy's mother. With no injury to the integrity of the text, think of which family member appeals to a boy who is being beaten by the harsh realities of wild living. Who is most likely to come to the mind of a boy whose stomach has been wrinkled by hunger and his taste buds dulled by the sight of slop? Whose embrace will truly console a young man, who has clearly brought shame upon the pride of his family? Mother's gentleness can erase any harshness the world brings. Just the smell of Mother's cooking would bring life to dead taste buds, and relief to a troubled stomach. Mother's embrace would solidify any redemption that father may initiate.

From the pigpen, the prodigal helps us to see that a sense of family can be physically fulfilling. Our families are incubators of the physical world before they are anything. Our families help us to understand the physical world, as well as how to be stewards of the physical world. A sense of family provides for us all an outlook on the world that helps us to benefit from it. I once interacted with a family that followed the horses. Every piece of money they came in contact with ended up feeding some horse. Yet, even that gambling afflicted family possessed a sense of what is physically necessary for survival. Families teach us the necessity of food, clothing, and health care.

It doesn't matter where you go in life, you will have to eat, sleep, be clean, and take care of yourself. No amount of money eliminates the need for basic physical upkeep. Likewise, no matter how broke you get the need for physical fulfillment remains. You can party for as long as you want, but you can't party long without eating and sleeping. And you will party alone, if you don't clean yourself up.

The young man in a pigpen came to his senses and recognized the physical fulfillment provided by family. "I can join in the physical processes that make life wholesome. I will work with my family, join in with the servants. I need not starve in a pigpen, when family life can be so fulfilling."

Finally, the young man in the pigpen helps us to see that a sense of family can be spiritually liberating. Long before the boy had physically left home, he had spiritually left home. His transgressions against family began while he was in the family. The spiritual bankruptcy of this lad actually took place long before his money ran out. There in a pigpen, down and out, he recognizes that sins against family are in fact sins against God. "Father, I have sinned against heaven and against you. I am no longer worthy to be called your son; make me like one of your hired servants."

The pigpen realities of our lives can be traced to sins against our families. It matters little how dysfunctional we may label our families. All families are "born in sin and shaped in iniquity." All families are a part of God's original intention to create community, where people can live out meaningful lives in harmony with brothers and sisters. All families are spiritual incubators where the language of love is taught, where the ethics of acceptance is cultivated, and where the vision of community is cast.

There are some things about our families we may not like. In fact, there may be some things wrong with our families that not even God likes. But our families belong to us. If God would have wanted to shape me in another family, he would have given me another family. God saw fit to place me with "the Bernstines," and use me as His child.

God uses the family to spiritually instruct us. God uses parents to teach us about the love of God. God uses children to teach us about the citizenship of heaven. God uses brothers and sisters to teach us about discipleship. God uses home as a seminary to teach us the power of prayer and the witness of the Bible. God uses our dining rooms to teach us about the blessedness of daily bread.

Let us not be hard on our families, for God uses prodigal sons and wayward daughters to teach us the power of forgiveness and the willingness of God to redeem. God uses adulterous wives to teach us that "all have sinned and come short of God's glory" and no one can cast a stone. God uses weak husbands to show us the strength of faithful women. God uses His only begotten Son to show us His Fatherly love.

Jesus faced hardships, but He never quit.
Jesus faced problems, but He never gave up.
Jesus faced disappointments, but He never surrendered.
Jesus faced discouragements, but He never caved in.
Jesus carried burdens, but He never buckled under.
Jesus faced adversities, but He never forgot His
    commitments.

From the pigpen, we learn that no one is so low that He can never go home. No one is so out-of-it, that he/she cannot return to the family.

A VIEW OF THE FAMILY FROM
THE FIELD

Text: *"Now his older son was in the field. And as he came and drew near to the house, he heard music and dancing. So he called one of the servants and asked what these things meant. And he said, 'Your brother has come, and because he has received him safe and sound, your father has killed the fatted calf.' But he was angry and would not go in. Therefore his father came out and pleaded with him. So he answered, 'Lo, these many years I have been serving you; I never transgressed your commandment at any time; and yet you never gave me a young goat, that I might make merry with my friends. But as soon as this son of yours came, who has devoured your livelihood with harlots, you killed the fatted calf for him.' And he said to him, 'Son, you have always been with me, and all that I have is yours. It was right that we should make merry and be glad, for your brother was dead and is alive, and was lost and is found.'"*
*(**Luke 15:25-32,** New King James Version)*

Among the many obvious truths about the nature and quality of family that we so often take for granted is: the glaring differences among family members. Most of us have erroneously assumed that just because persons are of the same family lineage they ought to act the same, be the same, see things the same way, and approach life the same. I shall never forget the concluding look that came across my mother's face, nor the tone of her voice when she declared: "It's something having to deal with all the different personalities of my children." I was but a teenage boy, when Mamma sighed those words. However, no words that she has ever spoken have been so deeply planted in my mind. There she was, barely thirty years old, with the huge task of adequately parenting eight children, four boys and four girls, with me as her third child.

Mamma's words have been pivotal in my approach to

parenting and pastoring, basically in dealing with people period. Mamma's words always shatter any sinful attempt of mine to try and lump people into some comfortable generality. Whenever I try to package people into a single group, in order to make life more comfortable for me, I am always shaken from my illusions and must confess: "It's something having to deal with all the different personalities of [Hagar's] children."

One need give only casual attention to the Biblical witness to see God's unique stamp upon each created personality. The Bible lifts out in page after page that common parental and family formation does not produce people who are just alike. There was only one Cain and one Abel. There may have been more than one person named Enoch, but only one walked with God without ever tasting death. There was only one Noah, one Shem, one Ham, and one Japheth. There was only one Abraham, one Lot, one Sarah, one Hagar, one Rebecca, one Rachel, one Leah. There was only one Isaac, one Jacob, one Esau, one Reuben, one Simeon, one Levi, one Dan, one Naphtali, one Gad, one Asher, one, Zebulun, one Joseph, and one Benjamin. One Moses rises up to set the captives free. One Joshua commissioned to claim the Promised Land. The list goes on; endless are the uniquenesses of our humanity. Paul said, "God has made of one blood all nations...."

Mamma seems to have tapped into what God had known all the time, "It's something having to deal with all the different personalities of my children."

In the midst of all of our uniqueness there flows a common blood. There is something that binds us closer than we care to acknowledge, and much closer than we care to accept. We are on one hand most unique. On the other hand, however, we are bound by the awful fact that none of us was born inside of Eden. We are all descendants of a universal tragedy. The powerful presence of sin has been as much us, as the air we breathe. All born of the seed of men, and from the womb of women, have been born in sin and shaped in iniquity. My name may be different. My birth date may personalize me. My experiences may make me somewhat unique. But just as sure as I have been born, I share the common reality of human imperfection.

When I reread the so-called story of the Prodigal Son, I was humbled by its message for our families. Two sons of common family lineage, but very different in their approaches to life, and their understanding of family. They were both born from the same parents. They both lived in the same house, and as boys played in the same yard. They both shared in the work around the house, until the younger son got tired of it. They both ate the same food, drank water from the same wells, and probably wore similar clothing. They both attended the same schools, most likely had the same teachers. They both attended the same synagogue and listened to the same rabbi preach the same sermon. With all of their common experiences these two sons were totally different.

One was older than the other. One son left home, and rejected all that his family had valued and taught. One stayed home and accepted the family rules and the parental discipline. One took all he had and splurged it on loose living. The other held on to his, by letting it remain in the family treasure. One was wild and careless, finally hitting the bottom and becoming a homeless slave, who slopped hogs for the enemy of his family's values. The other was quite careful. He wasted nothing. He was steady and stable, trustworthy and responsible.

The differences in these two boys are striking until the younger son returns from his rendezvous with pigpen living. When the younger son returned from his wild escapades, the true nature of the older son came to surface. With all of his steadiness and stability, carefulness and trustworthiness, he was literally worse off than his brother. Sin had seized his spirit in such a way that it distorted his perception of what a family was all about. From the position of the field, the older son failed to see that the grace-filled reality of family keeps the door open for the tragic wanderings of prodigal sons, wayward daughters, prodigal wives, and unruly husbands. He failed to see the obvious fact that the family is a reservoir of grace.

No one deserves to live in family. Family was created from the love of God, who designed that none would live alone. We are all here by the grace of God. Sin may have made the entry of some of us less than conventional, but God allowed us to get here. No one votes to be born. No one is given the privilege, not normally, to pick and choose who your parents will be. No one has any say in who their brothers and sisters will be, nor how they will turn out. Family is God's premier expression of grace, for family illustrates the basic expectations of living in harmony with others, who are as different from us as they are like us.

Without family, we would never have acquired the capacity for speech. Without family, we would have never became acquainted with fundamental human rights. We would have learned nothing about sharing, giving and receiving; caring, living and loving. No family is perfect, because all families are composed of imperfect people. The reality of sin, within the lives of the individual family members, makes perfect family life impossible. The elder son disturbed me because he unveiled the true tragedy of so many of our families, that as a consequence has devastated God's vision of a redemptive community. We can never truthfully talk about a harmonious church, while giving no attention to the hell in our homes. Our churches are composed of the same people who live in our homes. What sin does in the home shows up at church.

From the elder son's perspective, family life was something we earn. Out of his own mouth, he reveals that family is for "none but the righteous." Listen, as he blasts his father for opening the door of reconciliation to his brother: "Lo, these many years I have served, and I have never disobeyed your command; yet you never gave me a kid, that I might make merry with my friends." His words reek the kind of demonic selfishness that will wreck any family. Family, for him, evolved around him. He built up a view of the family that was dependent upon what he did. If the family was to ever make merry, it must come out of what he does and what he wants.

How tragic a view of the family! But is it not the common trend of many of our families? A lot of us think that our family rises and falls on us. We, men, don't think a family is whole without us. Sisters! You say it all the time. "A woman's work is never done." This left-field, far-out, off-base perspective continues to destroy any potential for merriment in our homes. If one person thinks he/she makes the family happen, he/she will forever be unhappy, angry, and unsatisfied. Moreover, when families turn inward and are concerned only for themselves, those families are in conflict with God's will.

As he continued angrily berating his father, he revealed further deteriorations of his spirit. "But when this son of yours came, who has devoured your living with harlots, you killed for him the fatted calf!" He not only thought that the family was something you earned, but he viewed the family as having no room for failures. He had literally exempted his brother from his heart. He never refers to the younger as his brother; he's referred to as "your son." It appears that the elder son used the differences between him and his brother to build barriers that divided. He used the brother's failures as grounds for eternal rejection. As far as he was concerned, the young man was no longer a member of the family. He viewed the family as courtroom to make judgments, about who was worthy of the father's favor. He viewed the family in alienating ways, where once one left there was no coming back.

The elder son's view of family reveals that prodigality works both ways. We can be just as prodigal at home, as we can be away from home. We can be just as destructive of family in all of our rightness, as we can be in our wrongness. We can be just as far from God in the church, as we can be outside of the church. We can be as detrimental to the family at home, as we can be away from home.

But, I thank God someone else was in the field. I thank God there were some other words spoken in the field. The Other in the field helps us to see a more redemptive view of the family. Just as the father ran down the road to greet his humbled, homecoming son; the same father runs toward the field to entreat his angry, arrogant, homebound son. To the angry son, he speaks; "Son, you are always with me, and all that I have is yours."

Through the actions and words of the Father, we are privileged to see that the family is a gift to all. God gives us family, and we are individual gifts to our family. The family is just filled with gifts, because the family is a gift. The family is God's gift to humanity. We come into our families with built-in differences. Yet, God uses our families to teach us acceptance. God uses our families as tools for our creation. God uses our families to teach us patience. God uses our families to build us up in endurance. God uses our families to give us character. God uses our families to help us understand trust. God uses our families to give us the gifts of faith, hope, and love. Our families provide us with an opportunity to participate in a past and a future, that we never physically visit. No greater gift, other than salvation in Jesus, can one have than family. The most important things in life can be received in the family. "All that the family has is ours."

God wants us to see the family as a gift, so that we may become gift-bearers. Only when we give to the health and wholeness of our family can we ever appreciate what God is trying to do with the family. The family ultimately belongs to God. God created it. God has kept our families. God has blessed us to be family. We should praise God for the gift of family.

Through the actions and words of the father, we are privileged to see that the family, in all of its giftedness, can bring grief to all. The elder son's hurts were probably expressions of the hurt he felt when brother left home. He probably grieved when his only brother left home ahead of him, and without him. I can recall being devastated when my oldest sister left home. Something left our family, when she went out on her own. If it hurts when family members leave to do good, Oh, how it hurts when they leave to do bad.

The father recognized and accepted the fact that his son had left and wasted himself. The language he used describes the depth of his son's wanderings. "Your brother was dead,...he was lost." The son had been literally considered destroyed, perished, useless, totally ruined. He was numbered among those who had ceased to live, departed from life. His actions had rendered him destitute, no longer considered as one who lived. He was a dead brother, a lost brother.

The pain the son brought to his family was not being ignored. It hurts when family members go astray. It does something to the whole family when one member falls short, fails, misses the mark. Let no one cover this up: It hurts when family members make fools of themselves, ruin their lives in wild and loose living. Yet, the truth must be told that all of our families have at least one wayward member. However, notwithstanding, but, nonetheless, he is our brother. She is our sister. He is my father. She is our mother. That is our family member. Therefore, redemption is possible. If he/she seeks reconciliation, the door stands ajar. If she is seriously repentant, and wants to rejoin the family, a place has been reserved for her. In the words of the songwriter, "He ain't heavy, he's my brother. She ain't heavy, she's my sister."

In conclusion, the father helps us to see that the family can provide joy for all. The father says, "It was fitting to make merry and be glad." In other words, making merriment over the return of your brother was the family thing to do. C. E. McLain has brought to our attention that when someone dies, or is sick, we will hurriedly bring pies, chickens, pots of this and pots of that. We are quick to help people in their grief and trouble. Truly, this is the family thing to do. Another side of our family responsibility is to rejoice when something good happens to one another. The family thing to do when someone gets a raise is to rejoice. The family thing to do when someone gets a new car, or a new house is to rejoice. We should not get jealous or angry, we should rejoice.

No other occasion should bring us more joy than when some prodigal son, or wandering daughter, finds her way back home. The truth be told, when one of our members is made whole it makes us more whole. When one of our members becomes alive, it enlivens us all. When one of our members finds him/herself, we find a little more of ourselves. When one of our members is lifted up, we all are elevated a little higher. When one of our members is straightened out, we all get a little straighter. When the way gets easier for one of us, the way gets easier for all of us. Vance Havner has said that "Too many Christians are content with cheese and crackers, thus, they never enter the banquet." I don't know about you, but I have made up my mind that I'm going in. The joy is not in the field, but joy is on the inside. I've made up my mind, when some-one comes home, I will praise His holy name. The reason I'm going to praise His name is, because I know the song and the dance.

I once was lost was lost, but now I'm found.
I was blind, but now I see.
I was dead, but now I'm alive.
In Jesus, I'm alive.
In His love, I'm alive.
In His mercy, I'm alive.
In His grace, I'm alive.
In His family, I'm alive.

SPRINKLE BLOOD ON THE FAMILY DOORPOST

Text: *"Then Moses called all the elders of Israel, and said to them, 'Select lambs for yourselves according to your families, and kill the passover lamb. Take a bunch of hyssop and dip it in the blood which is in the basin, and touch the lintel and the two doorposts with the blood which is in the basin; and none of you shall go out of the door of his house until the morning. For the Lord will pass through to slay the Egyptians; and when he sees the blood on the lintel and on the two doorposts, the Lord will pass over the door, and will not allow the destroyer to enter your houses to slay you.' "* (***Exodus 12:21-23,*** Revised Standard Version)

A few years ago, the world was fastened to the television screen by the unbelievable tragedy of an exploding space shuttle. We watched replay after replay of the tragic misfortune. Slow motion replays impacted our minds and memories. To convenience a curious world, death was dramatized in endless replay. NASA, and many others, were concerned about the technological implications that the shuttle's destruction was threatening. Scientist, politicians, and astronauts were concerned about the viability of future space projects. Questions were raised: Is it safe to continue with business as usual? Are we comfortable enough to continue risking human lives, professional and civilian? Such were the questions that dominated the technological arena.

As I viewed replay after replay, another concern rattled my spirit. I became deeply concerned about the families of those tragically lost in the explosion. I anguished over the fact that technology, politics, and science dominated the center of world concerns. A tragic fact was relegated to secondary concerns: that when the shuttle blew up, a husband lost a wife, a wife lost a husband, children lost parents. A mother lost a daughter, or a son. A father lost a son, or a daughter. The real tragedy of the space shuttle was not scientific. The real tragedy was that when the space ship blew up, some families blew up—destroyed, never to be the same again.

Oh, I am certain that most of you shared in the grief of those devastated families. We, all, at least remotely suffered with them. However, I am disturbed about our apathetic acceptance of daily explosions that occur in our midst. Explosions of massive proportion take place in urban settings all across America. Seven families, destroyed in space, seem to touch us more deeply than the millions of family explosions right in our midst.

A recent documentary entitled, "The Vanishing Family," depicted some of the darksome causes of black families being blown asunder. We seemingly have accepted it as a way of life for teenagers to produce most of our children, when most of them are too immature to care for themselves. A family explosion! We seem to have accepted it as a way of life for young men to father children, without first becoming a man. A family explosion! We need to tell our young males that a boy can make a baby, but it takes a man to be a father.

Have we accepted as a way of life for drugs, lottery, numbers, and crime to be the economic strongholds of the black community? Have we accepted as a way of life for our young males to stand on the corner, being "cool", with an "OPP" (other people's problems) philosophy about life; while our communities decay in our hands? A family explosion daily devastates the black community.

Yes, I grieved over the tragedy of the astronauts' families. But, I cry daily tears over the continuing tragedy of the Black family explosion. If we are not careful we will raise up a generation, who will neither know nor respect the Black family tradition. The work of our Family Emphasis month will be to bring to the forefront some of the many struggles of the Black family. A meaningful menu of events has been prepared for us so that we can reflect upon our plight. To begin the challenge, which I pray will forever endure, I suggest we begin by sprinkling blood on the family doorpost. We begin by looking afresh at the Exodus story for biblical clues to liberation.

Today's text offers a fascinating challenge to the Christian family. The Israelites stood one plague away from structural bondage. Liberation from the political and economical shackles of Egypt was but a few hours away. The faith challenge of the Red Sea awaited them. They stood with their bags packed, walking canes in hand, and with travelling on their minds. The Promised Land awaited their arrival; but, first, they must sprinkle blood on the family doorpost.

Recently at Vanderbilt Divinity School, Albert Rabateou made a powerful and thought provoking statement. As he explicated the historical meaning of the Book of Exodus in the lives of Black Americans, he said, "America has always meant one thing to White Americans and something else to Black Americans. For White Americans America represented Canaan Land, or the Promised Land. For Black Americans, America has always been the epitome of oppressive Egypt." Our foreparents seem to have had a better grasp of this truth, so they sang in the belly of Egypt-America:

Go down Moses, And tell Ol' Pharaoh,
To let my people Go.

Our tragedy may well be that we have come to believe ourselves residents of Canaan, when we are actually in Egypt. We have confused Egypt with Canaan Land. Yes, maybe the physical structures of bondage have been eased; maybe we are on the brink of political and economical liberation; maybe the faith-challenge of a Red Sea awaits us up the road; and, I am certain that a good number of us stand with bags packed, walking canes in hand, and with travelling on our minds. But, we must first sprinkle blood on the family doorpost.

Upon reading the text, I literally discovered some truths necessary for family salvation. Within the text are enough essentials for the Black church to rededicate itself to the salvation of the Black family. God has some good news for us, in the midst of our bad news situation. We, as a part of the historical Black church, stand within the gates of the Black family salvation. This is no new task. The Black church has always provided the soul and heart of strong Black families. Move with me through the dynamics of our text.

Verse 21 reads: "Then Moses called all the elders of Israel, and said to them, 'Select lambs for yourselves according to your families, and kill the passover lamb.'" For you who have ears to hear, God had ordered Moses and consequently passed down the orders to the people, in particular, to obedient men.

God gives orders to leaders so that he/she might give them to God's people. God is an order-giving God.

One of the great tragedies of our people is the blatant disregard for authority. We simply find it difficult obeying orders, particularly, Black orders! Too many of us want to do what we want to do. I know I have said this no few times at Olivet, but every day I am faced by folk who insist on disregarding authority. The implications for our families ought to be quite clear. If our children , our husbands, or our wives, see us habitually disobeying God, by our disregard for church leadership, why should they obey us? If we are so satanically smart that we can rationalize disobedience in the church, why surely our family members can formulate reasons to disobey us. Disobedience breeds disobedience, and disobedience destroys families.

What has disobedience to do with blood and doorpost? What a marvelous question to ask. Blood, simply put, represents life. Doorpost, simply stated, represents those support beams that stand at the entrances and exits of life. Doorposts are visible beams and lintels are the hidden beams. (Lord, I wish I could make it plain.) Blood, or life, on the doorpost represents what is essential to sustenance of life.

Obedience to God is essential to life. God, as giver of life, willingly sustains us when we are obedient to His will. For the most part, obedience is a visible sign. Somebody sees our acts of obedience, as well as our acts of disobedience. Obedience is blood on the doorpost! There runs throughout the Bible, according to Gardner Taylor, a scarlet stream of blood evidenced by obedience, much of which is family-oriented:

Children— "Honor your father and mother...."

Parents— "Do not provoke your children to anger, but bring them up in the discipline and instruction of the Lord."

Wives —"Submit to your husbands..." (I Peter focuses, "to your own husband...."

Husbands—"Submit to your wives...." "Be husband of one wife...."

The book of Ephesians gives a broader and much more inclusive Christian perspective: " Be subject to one another out of reverence for Christ." If present any church hard-heads, I Peter 5:5 says, "You that are younger be subject to the elders. Clothe yourselves, all of you, with humility toward one another, for God opposes the proud, but gives grace to the humble." God rewards family obedience. Obedience is blood on the doorpost!

In verse 22, Moses tells them exactly where to place the blood and how to place the blood. " Touch the lintel and the doorposts...and none of you shall go out of the house until the morning." I can hardly run past the last portion of the verse. Listen again, "and none of you shall go out of the house until the morning." It certainly appears that the Lord wants the people to stay in the house. In this getting-out-of-the-house age, our redemption has much to do with staying in the house. Stay in the family! Oh, if our young people, who aimlessly roam the streets going into one thing and then another, would just stay in the house. Certainly the house needs to be worth staying in, but many of our neighborhood ills could be alleviated by some constructive staying in the house.

Our evangelistic thrust and efforts are to get people to stay in the house. The church's witness has been unnecessarily weakened by folk leaving the house. People join today and are gone tomorrow. People need to stay in God's house! If our families are to survive the death angels of our time, they must take seriously God's Word to stay in the house. If drugs and drink, crime and "pen" time, sex and sensationalism, illiteracy and illegitimacy, cults and creeps are to destroy our people, it will happen because we refuse to stay in the house. We need to stay in the family-house and in the church-house, or the drug-house, the whorehouse, and the jailhouse will be our house. Everyday we need to do all we can to tell somebody, "you better stay in the house."

In verse 23, Moses informed the people why they must do what they must do. He told them, "For the Lord will pass through to slay the Egyptians; and when he sees blood on the lintel and on the two doorposts, the Lord will pass over the door, and will not allow the destroyer to enter your house and slay you." In other words, if we do not do as the Lord commands, we will die with the Egyptians. To disobey God would, in essence, identify us with those who are in direct and deadly contradiction to God's will. Our very life is at stake. Our future depends on it. Our existence is contingent upon blood being sprinkled on the doorpost.

Notice, the concern was not for individuals. The concern was for the people. The concern was not just for Moses and his family. The concern was for the entire Israelite people. We have too many folk concerned only about me, myself, and I. If life-saving blood is to ever be on our doorpost, it must be for the people. We must come to grips with the fact that the destruction of one family threatens the life of all families. Somewhere I read, "Every divorce destroys a small civilization." The destroyer might visit my house today, but he will visit yours tomorrow. We must become more people-minded and less self-indulgent. A concern for others is putting blood on the doorpost.

Families are destroyed by selfishness. Sin is selfishness and selfishness is sin. Parents must not be selfish with their children. No family should be so self-centered that it ignores the worth of others. My little too-goody family will not help this bad world. Any family dominated by a selfish spirit is but a few days and full of trouble. Every child is a unique personality, with a unique personhood independent of other persons. No few parents have painfully pushed children out of the house by imposing their limited ideas and narrow perspectives on the lives of their children. We need to quit putting emotional and psychological chains on our children. We need to respect our children, if our children are to respect us. A respect for the uniqueness of our children moves us beyond the limiting binds of selfishness. A concern for the blessedness of other people represents a sprinkling of blood on the doorpost.

Verses 25-27a speak of a coming future. Moses, along with the people, saw beyond their space and time. They sensed a future, in which they would participate only in the memory of their children.

Oh, how we need to see beyond our space and time! Oh, that we, as a people, even as a congregation, would only grasp the coming future! None of us is here to stay. We are all slowly marching off the scene. What will our children have to say about us? Or, will they even want to remember us? It may be that we will be best forgotten. Are we committed to investing today for our children's tomorrow? Or, will there be any children for tomorrow?

If it means anything to anyone, beside myself, the church lives on a future-oriented faith. Yes, "faith is the substance of things hoped for and the evidence of worlds not seen." Blood on the doorpost looks for tomorrow; it lives for the morning.

The people consented to do as instructed, but before they departed they bowed down and worshiped. When they considered what the Lord was about to do, they bowed their heads and worshiped. Allow me to interject, that whenever a people obey the Lord they are essentially bowing down and worshiping. Whenever a people connect as a people, over individual inclinations, that is a step toward bowing down and worshiping. Whenever a people will sacrifice for the future, that's bowing down and worshiping. Furthermore, whenever a people tell the story of what God has done for them, that's bowing down and worshiping.

The Bible says, "the people bowed their heads and worshiped." Then they went and did what the Lord commanded.

Well, what about us? What are we going to do? Are we going to obey the Lord? Are we going to come together, as a people with a purpose? Are we going to guarantee ourselves a future? Are we willing to sacrifice? Are we willing to sprinkle blood on the family doorpost?

> *What can wash our sins away?*
> *Nothing but the blood of Jesus.*
> *What can make our families whole again?*
> *Nothing but the blood of Jesus?*
> *What can cleanse our homes?*
> *Nothing but the blood of Jesus.*
> *What can give peace in the community?*
> *Nothing but the blood of Jesus.*
> *What can make us love everybody?*
> *Nothing but the blood of Jesus.*

THE WALL AND THE GATES

Text: *"The words of Nehemiah the son of Hacaliah. Now it happened in the month of Chislev, in the twentieth year, as I was in Susa the capital, that Hanani, one of my brethren, came with certain men out of Judah; and I asked them concerning the Jews that survived, who had escaped exile, and concerning Jerusalem. And they said to me, 'The survivors there in the province who escaped exile are in great trouble and shame; the wall of Jerusalem is broken down, and its gates are destroyed by fire.'"*

"Then I said to them, 'You see the trouble we are in, how Jerusalem lies in ruins with its gates burned. Come, let us build the wall of Jerusalem, that we may no longer suffer disgrace.' And I told them of the hand of my God which had been upon me for good, and also of the words which the king had spoken to me. And they said, 'Let us rise up and build.' So they strengthened their hands for the good work. But when Sanballat the Horonite and Tobiah the servant, the Ammonite, and Geshem the Arab heard of it, they derided us and despised us and said, 'What is this thing that you are doing? Are you rebelling against the king? Then I replied to them, 'The God of heaven will make us prosper, and we his servants will arise and build; but you have no portion or right or memorial in Jerusalem.'"
(Nehemiah 1:1-3;2:17-20)

What makes us who we are are those experiences which we share in common. Americans share a common history, a common heritage. A virtually young nation, brash and bold, born on the wings of some high ideal: "as self-evident that all men are created equal, and that they have been endowed with certain inalienable rights and among them are life, liberty, and the pursuit of happiness." This ideal has been held high by the nation's people. Interestingly, the same nation allowed and upheld a system of oppression unequaled in modern history. The system of slavery, as perpetuated in America, has few rivals in the history of civilized people.

It is out of this history that Blacks, particularly Black Americans, are the common sharers of a unique history. We are who we are because of what we share in common. What makes us who we are are those experiences that we share. God has strangely used us, and still wants to use us, to reveal to the world the power of the gospel. I listened in on a preacher's prayer, a moving conversation with God. He announced that "we are who we are because God is who God is." No one can fully explain why God wants to use us as endurers of slavery, Jim Crow, institutional racism, and as hammers of civil rights. Only God knows, therefore, let us be receptive to God's ideals.

The people of Israel are who they are because God is who God is. The drama of history has so often found them in strange and uncomfortable situations. Painful appointments were divinely arranged to be in Egypt, the wilderness, fiery furnaces, lion's dens, and Babylonian exiles. Their responses to the challenges of God are sacrificially etched throughout the biblical story.

The story of Nehemiah was told on the ash heap of the Babylonian Exile. Foreign forces had completely disrupted a once proud nation. The community was ruined by the devastating assaults of unfriendly foes and angry forces. All that had once made the people who they were was on the brink of total annihilation. The family structure was hardly recognizable. Businesses were non-existing, thus non-profitable. The educational systems that once shaped minds for the future were shambled ruins. To worsen an already desperate situation, the ordinances of God were fading from memory. The power of the promise had weakened and waned.

It was to this kind of situation that a Nehemiah emerged. Nehemiah was a privileged person, who spent his days within the comforts of society. His diet was of the presumptuous "haves" and not that of the poorly "have-nots."

His wardrobe was fashionable. He wore not the garments of poverty. He was daily decorated with privilege and prosperity. However, Nehemiah never allowed the frills of society to blind him to the treasured scenes from whence he had come. He knew who he was, thus, the stuff of society did not create him. He kept in constant contact with the people of his heritage and history.

One day he got the news from home that the people were in bad shape. They were in great pain and were being treated with dreadful shame. Their plight was pitiful. Their situation was sickening. Their life was loathsome. The community was depressing, trouble on every hand. Difficulties were mounting, anxieties on an increase, disgraces were many, and distresses compound. In essence, the people had emerged out of slavery but they were no better off. And to make matters worse, the wall of Jerusalem was broken down. What made the people distinct and unique lay in total ruin.

Well, what about us? I sensed that for Black Americans the wall is down. Those structures that once enclosed us, supported us and protected us— they are down! Without the walls of family and faith, we are vulnerable to every evil and ill-meaning influence. Our uniqueness risks being eliminated by the on-rushing forces of conformity. What once supported us and held us up, and held us together, now lies in shambles, exposed to every unfriendly element. Without the strength of the walls, we are noticeably weakened and susceptible to the mocking winds of disgrace and shame. Nothing else really matters, without the walls. Therefore, someone needs to look at the walls.

Now, before we look at the correct walls, we need to eliminate some of these bad walls. There are some walls in our lives that we need to eliminate. Yes, there are some walls we need to tear down. I speak of the walls of selfishness that separate us from one another. I speak of the walls of pettiness that hinder us from sacrificial accomplishments. I speak of the fortresses of fear that dare only to peek out and shout out. I speak of the walls of envy, distrust, jealousy, and self-hatred. We need to tear these walls down!

The walls of greed, self-gratification, phoniness and foolishness. We need to tear down the walls that hinder us from caring, loving, forgiving, and understanding. The walls that perpetuate self-destruction and mass genocide—these walls need to be torn down and kept down.

We do not need a crash course in sociology to make us aware of the ruins within the Black community. None but the totally naive and ridiculously stupid will deny that our people are living in social ruins. The evidence is everywhere, even within our church. Our own memories will reveal to us that people are in worst shape now than they were back "then." Too few of us, like Nehemiah, are privileged and prosperous. As a people, we are hurting because certain crucial walls have been torn down.

Jim Bevels, a former aide of the late Martin Luther King, Jr., shared with me the essentials of a strong community. He told me that the primary components of a viable community are five-fold: the family, the school, the marketplace (or business), the clinic, and the church. It is quite obvious that the walls and gates of our communities now lie in ruins. The very gates, in the form of broken down family structures, meaningless school systems, unsupported businesses, unhealthy medical facilities, and irrelevant churches are being destroyed by the flames of hell.

Why is it that we are so vulnerable to the lecherous efforts of every parasitic politician? Why is it that we lack an economic base to finance our future? What do we see as the primary reason for poor health within the Black community? Tell me, why are so few of our children excited about education? And, why are we so susceptible to the religious tricks of every Bible-toting quack? It appears that Jim Jones is not really dead, he just put on a different suit and got on television. Our vulnerability, our instability, and our susceptibility are the results of torn down walls and burnt-down gates.

How then shall we respond to the widespread devastations within our communities? If the Black community is to overcome its troubles and rise above the shambles of shame, we must rebuild the walls and gates of our communities. Our families must be strengthened. We must reassume the responsibility of educating our children, as well as reeducate ourselves. We must begin to patronize our own businesses, supporting one another. The concerns of health must leave politics and return to the people. We must encourage young people to address the urgency of self-preservation through health care. We must quit playing with God's church, using it as a theater for trivialities. The church is for the building of God's kingdom on earth, as it is in heaven.

As I continued to read the admirable story of Nehemiah, I was disturbingly impressed by his response to the challenge. Nehemiah suggests to us that the rebuilding of the walls and gates never happens as long as we take refuge within the illusionary comforts of the palace. Brothers and Sisters, we must be willing to get away from what we think we have and return to what we know we have. The false world must be released, if the real world is to be rebuilt. Did not the prophet warn, "Woe to them that are at ease in Zion." As long as the walls and gates are down, we are not really safe, even with fancy bars and gun barrels.

Since the walls and gates lie in ruins, it is highly suggestive of a call to work. If the walls and gates of our community are to ever be rebuilt, we must quit so much playing and start working. Sad it is that we live in an age that abhors hard work. The Devil has deceived us into believing that hard work has no worthwhile merit. I often notice the workers on construction sites. I notice white men working heavy machines, supervising, even shoveling and laying gravel. Several yards from the labor, I notice the brothers waving orange flags and directing the traffic. These same brothers leave the job and brag among the community, "I don't work hard. All I do is wave an orange flag. I got it made." Such a perspective may answer the question of escalating unemployment among black males, for how many people want to hire somebody who only knows how to wave a flag?

If the walls and gates are to be rebuilt, we must commit ourselves to hard work. If we want to be compensated for efforts expended, we must be willing to work. The Lord has said, "Work while it is day, the night comes when no man can work."

Rebuilding the walls and gates are also a call to discipline. In Proverbs 10:17, "He who heeds instruction is on the path of life, but he who rejects reproof goes astray." It is also written, "spare the rod, spoil the child." Too many of our folk are spoiled because the rod of reproof has been spared. People who reject discipline are usually destructive, and not constructive. The walls and gates are to be built a certain way and not just any kind of way. Education can be defined as structured discipline.

The majority of Nehemiah's people went to work. The ruins of the walls and gates were perceived as a communal responsibility. Every one had to chip in and share the load. The rebuilding of our walls and our gates is everyone's responsibility. We all must share the load, and shoulder responsibility. There is a job for everyone of us, from the least to the greatest. No one person can rebuild our broken down walls, nor restore our burned down gates. No one person, not even Jesus, can bear all of our crosses. We must responsibly bear our own cross.

Lest we be too naive in our work, the call to rebuild is also an invitation for trouble. Sanballat the Horonite, and Tobiah the Ammonite, along with Geshem the Arab, rallied to cause trouble for the workers. They caused Nehemiah and the cause of rebuilding trouble. As the people rebuilt the walls and restored the gates, trouble arose from forces within and without. Trouble sought to discourage the work.

Brothers and Sisters, difficulties will come. Troubles will rise. In fact, difficulties are a part of the landscape of progress. It is foolish of us to believe that life is trouble-free, particularly when engaged in the reconstruction of a people. Progressive living and successful living never come without trials and tribulations. J. Wallace Hamilton once noted, "life was never made to run smoothly." Someone has said, " Into each life some rain must fall."

I thank God for the rains of life. Without the rains, the grass would not grow, flowers would not bloom, and refreshment would not come. Dr. C. A. W. Clark has stated, "All sunshine makes a desert." Thank God for the rain.

As Nehemiah and company rebuilt the walls, and continued restoring the gates the Bible says, "they worked with a tool in one hand and a sword in the other." In other words, they used one hand to build and the other hand to protect. One hand for construction and the other hand for protection. One hand for progress and the other hand for defense.

Brothers and Sisters, too many of us have empty hands. Too many of us, if our hands are not empty, we are using them to destroy and disrupt. If we are not building and protecting, we are neglecting and tearing down. It is time to get a tool in one hand, and the sword of truth in the other hand.

Nehemiah reveals to us the proper way to rebuild the walls and to restore the gates. In verses 4-11, immediately after hearing of the wall and the gates, the Bible says, "when he heard these words he sat down and wept, and fasted and prayed for many days." If the wall is to be rebuilt and the gates restored, we will have to do as Nehemiah, get serious about the Lord. When God is taken seriously, the people of God go in prayer. The attitude of the serious is:

> *I love the Lord, because He heard my Cry;*
> *And pitied my evr'y groan.*
> *Long as I live, and troubles rise;*
> *I'll hasten to His throne.*

To rebuild the walls and restore the gates, we must humble ourselves and say:

> *Father, I stretch my hands to thee;*
> *No other help I know.*
> *If thou withdraw thyself from me,*
> *Oh, whither shall I go.*

NOW THAT WE ARE BLACK, NOW WHAT? REMEMBERING BY REMOVING

Text: *"You shall remember that you were a slave in the land of Egypt, and the Lord your God redeemed you; therefore I command you this today."* ***Deuteronomy 15:15***

One of the cruelest facts of slavery was the deliberate erasing of our history. The slave owners, or slave makers, intentionally deprived us of our roots. Since we were to be considered as animals, beasts of burden, a sense of history was supposedly not needed. So complete was this erasing process that our real names, languages, traditions, and heritage are now foreign to most of us. We have been so separated from the reality of our past that we laugh at the attempts to recover our roots. My three children will probably be victims of scorn, because Daddy and Mamma gave them names that point them away from falsity to their God-given destiny. Sad it is, that many "colored", "Negro", "Black", "Afro-Americans", now African Americans feel no warm kinship to the Mother Land.

If our disdain for Africa was all that we held in contempt, we might still possess an adequate sense of appreciable history. However, as a rule, we do not even appreciate and celebrate our painful, but promising, pilgrimage in America. People, not of our experience, both at home and abroad, have a deeper appreciation for the Black experience than we have. We appear to believe that being Black began in the sixties. Such an empty sense of history may well explain the apathy of our situation. But if the truth be told our history gives us clues to our destiny. Our history reveals our humanity. Embodied within our history are the vital essentials for forging a unity of spirit that will enable us to march forward. The pages of our history, here in America, reveal the real essence of Black Power.

James Cone, in his book <u>Black Theology and Black Power,</u> asserts that "Black Power is an attitude, an inward affirmation of the essential worth of blackness." So when I raise the question, "Now that we are Black, now what?", I am probing for the true measure of our value as persons, as a people. If being Black means something, it ought to be worth something. We ought to be able to place a value judgment on the experience of our Blackness. To say that we are Black is not enough. Being Black ought to be worth something. Cone continues, "to be human is to find some-thing worth dying for." Brothers and Sisters, if being Black does not shape our humanity, we don't really have any-thing worth living for. The truth is we are first human and then Black.

Within the historical archives of the venerable Fisk University Library, there lies a complete copy of the Slave Bible. Within the Slave Bible, we see evidences of evil's attempt to rob us of our humanity. Within the Slave Bible are no stories of the Exodus event; Moses' confrontation with Pharaoh; nor any of Jesus' words of the worth of each person and the value of freedom. Here we find the Bible being perverted to justify slavery, racism, and oppression. Religion has always been used to justify evil and to uphold oppression. Evil has always known that a religious lie told over and over again starts sounding like the truth.

The Slave Bible was the perpetuation of a religious lie that suggested that God was on the side of the Pharaohs, and not on the side of the folk in the brickyard. A religious lie tells people on slave row that God is blessing only the folk in the Big House. It is a lie that holds God up as God of the mansions, and not the mangers. However, the thread of consistency that weaves throughout the Biblical story is that the strong hand of God is always on the side of the weak. We hardly find a Biblical book where some refer-ence is not made to God's bringing the little people out of

Egypt. The Israelite people were greatly concerned that history preserve the story of their deliverance, even if they had to borrow other people's myths to convey it. They did not want any generation to ever forget from whence they come. They had a way of threading the Exodus into every fabric of society. Even marriages were solemnized with salvation history. Thus we hear repeatedly, "you shall remember that you were a slave in the land of Egypt, and the Lord your God redeemed you."

How many of us have a habit of sitting down with the family, the neighbors, and friends, and telling the story of our people? When was the last time you heard about a people being kidnapped, sold away from the shores of Africa; stacked in ships like inhuman cargo; suffered the bitter agony of the Middle Passage; sold into bondage, in a strange land; stripped of name and history; forced into slave labor; robbed of dignity; raped of virtue; manhood denied; womanhood brutalized; families liquidized; religion voodooized; and our total humanity demoralized? When was the last time your children heard the story? More importantly, when was the last time you told the story to them?

We cannot depend upon a Hollywood version of our story. We cannot even count on our schools to tell the story. No one ought to be able to tell our story like we can. Tarzan does not correctly portray Black folk. Indiana Jones, the Tarzan of the eighties, does not shed a decent light on our people. It is so much like the story of the monkey and the lion. According to the lion's version, the lion always eats the monkey. Now, if that is not the whole story; if it does not tell the monkey's version; well, the monkey ought to write some books. He ought to tell the story from the monkey's perspective. So it is with our people, we need to tell our own story.

Society has deceived us into being ashamed of our story. Some are fearful that our story might anger Blacks, rekindling a flame for vengeance. That is just another trick to rob us of our humanity. How can you be ashamed of your own history, particularly when it reveals the strong hand of God? Our story clearly reveals God using us, in spite of us. Furthermore, the story is not over yet.

The Israelites would tell their story anywhere. They are not waiting to return to Israel to tell it. When they met yesterday, in Nashville, Tennessee, they told the story once again. In response to the other point of deception, Blacks do not ordinarily breed vengeance. We are a passive people by nature, especially when we are at ourselves. Our recent displays of violence are largely attributed to external forces. We are not at ourselves. The overwhelming demons of drugs, drink, materialistic Americanism, and other forms of foolishness, clearly are enough to get us away from ourselves. The power of telling our own story has not been fully utilized.

Upon reading the book of Deuteronomy, I observed some suggestions for our restoration. I see some helpful hints that ought to give us impetus for positive direction. I see where a solid act of remembrance can free us to be what God intends for us to be.

The writing of our text is peculiarly located. God called the people to remember their servitude, especially in their relationships with one another. The story is: " If a slave is in your possession, allow him(her) their freedom on the seventh year. And when you let him(her) go, do not let him(her) go empty handed. But furnish him(her) liberally out of your own possessions." The call to remember was for the people not to get beside themselves; not to forget from whence they had come. In other words, by remembering they would remove any destructive illusions about themselves, others, and God.

Brothers and Sisters, we have a lot of illusions about Blackness. Illusions are erroneous perceptions about reality.

It is to see life in a way that is totally destructive. It is to see in life what is really not in life. It is to have a distorted vision of what life is really all about. What holds Black people in the present state of indecision, and communal loss of direction, is that too many of us have illusions about blackness. We are busy trying to live in a world that is not really here. Yes, illusions about blackness!

I am moved to believe that a proper memory of our slave heritage has the power to sober us, stabilize us, and to conceptualize our yearnings. A good memory can be a prime source for motivation. If we would just remember from whence we have come, we might start moving to where we ought to be going.

Allow me to list just a few of our illusions. We live an illusion if we think blackness of skin, alone, demands respect. To many of us are counting on skin color to see us through. Too many of us feel that the world owes us something just because we have black skin. Such a perception of blackness is to live an illusion. If Blackness, alone, will take you over, then go to the bank tomorrow and get a loan based on blackness. See if Blackness will be adequate collateral. Another illusion that has distorted many is the need to get down on others to make us feel like we are up. Many of us have to make others feel bad, so that we might feel good.

To equate our blackness on skin, alone, is to live a terrible illusion. Being black is not mere skin, it is an experience. The experience of who we are is forged out of the reality of our story. Our story is more than a skin color, it is the pride-filled determination of a people who are overcoming a tragic injustice on the human spirit.

The ridiculous attitude of being hard on ourselves, and on one another, is a terrible illusion. We ridiculously cut-up, cut-down, and rip-up one another. Then we stick out our ridiculous chests and say, "That's the way you treat a nigger—be hard on him/her." That is totally ridiculous! The white world has been too hard on us for us to perpetuate that illusion. It is an illusion to ridiculously put one another down in the name of being black. We need to lift one another up and hold one another up in the most positive light.

Another illusion of Blackness is that we have to do the ridiculous to be recognized and identified. Too many of us parade the ridiculous to establish our blackness. We talk loud and foolish. We can wear the most ridiculous clothes. We drive, grotesquely leaning, in some of the most ridiculous cars. (Then we wonder why the police stop us.) We think being stupid is smart, poor is virtuous, and to be mad and sad is to be glad. So much of what we do, even in the church, is utterly ridiculous. Another tragic illusion of Blackness is that we can only make it from the waist down. We are outrunning everybody. We are out-catching everybody. We are dunking and skying all over the basketball court. We have made art forms out of sporting events. We are out dancing everybody, no one can beat us sliding across the dance floor. We have even established ourselves as sexual olympiads, with gold medals in numerous bedrooms. A lot of our religion is from the waist down. We emphasize marching, hip swaying choirs, skirt-flying shouting, and holy rhythmic dancing. It is almost an established fact that no one can beat us from the waist down.

But, what about the heart up? There is more to blackness than running fast, jumping high, dancing slick, and loving long. It is an illusion to disregard the commitment of heart, the technology of hands, and the library of the mind. We are more than able to make it from the heart up, as well as from the waist down. Remembering from whence we have come helps us to embrace the completeness of our experience, thus, escaping the illusions of a partial black

50

experience. It is time for us to put more emphasis on the living from the heart up.

Another tragic illusion is to confuse the wilderness with the Promised Land. We still have a long way to go before experiencing the Promised Land. We have not yet arrived into the completeness of God's blessedness. Confusion about where we are reduces our capacity to engage in righteous struggle. It robs us of initiative for futuristic aspirations. To struggle the right struggle means denying ourselves and following Jesus. Too often our struggles are self-centered; as a consequence, we are immobilized from progress. Too much emphasis on instant gratification robs us of greater future benefits. God has more planned for us than food on the table, roofs over heads, clothing on backs, and other material niceties. The truth is obeying God's will and following God's beckoning makes us prime candidates to receive manna from heaven and water from rocks. God still wants to give us more than we can ever provide for ourselves. God still opens heavenly windows in the direction of the obedient.

The illusions of Blackness that render us into complacency and comfort are complete distortions. We must continue in the struggle, struggling the right struggle. Frederick Douglas once said, " If there is no struggle, there is no progress. Those who profess to favor freedom, and yet depreciate agitation, are [persons] who want crops without plowing up the ground. They want rain without thunder and lightning.... This struggle may be a moral one; or it may be a physical one; or it may be both moral and physical; but there must be a struggle."

The power of remembering can remove the illusions of Blackness. As the Lord spoke to Israel, the Lord yet speaks to us, " You shall remember that you were a slave in the land of Egypt, and the Lord your God redeemed you...." Notice, the removal of another illusion. The text says, "and the Lord your God redeemed you." It is an illusion to give credit to any other power, save the power of the Lord. Abraham Lincoln did not redeem us. He was merely a pawn in the hand of the Lord. Martin Luther King, Jr. did not redeem us. Why even Martin knew that he was just a servant in the hand of the Lord.

Brothers and Sisters, the Lord brought us out. The Lord redeemed us, and to be redeemed is to be restored. If we are to go anywhere from where we are, it will have be by the power of the Lord. I do not know, but it just may be that some of us question God's power. Some of us act as if we believe God has lost some power. If so, I pray for the shattering of that illusion, because the Lord still has all power in heaven and earth in His hand.

Why just this morning, the Lord separated light from darkness by the power of His hand. If God has lost some power, who then set the sun ablazing in the sky? If God has lost power, who spins the earth on Her equatorial axis? If God has lost some power, who set the stars shining in their silver sockets? It was the power of the Lord. If God has lost some power, you tell me then; who brings forth the rain, sleet, and snow? I know it was the power of the Lord.

By God's power, life is still given. Babies are still being born, by the power of the Lord. By God's power, I was awakened this morning and was able to start on my way. I know God still has all power; power to bring us out; power to lift us up; power to bring us through; power to redeem, restore, save and to keep. The Lord has power to forgive and forget. I know the Lord has all power, so I sing:

> *Guide me, O Thou great Jehovah*
> *Pilgrim thro' this barren land;*
> *I am weak, but thou art mighty,*
> *Hold me with thy powerful hand.*

AN UNUSUAL CONNECTION

Text: *"And immediately he left the synagogue, and entered the house of Simon and Andrew, with James and John. Now Simon's mother-in-law lay sick with a fever, and immediately they told him of her. And he came and took her by the hand and lifted her up, and the fever left her; and she served him."* (**Mark 1:29-31,** RSV)

Any savior worth worshiping at church ought to be worth serving at home. The reality is there exists too much religion that is good at church, but not worth a hill of beans at home. Included within this tragic dichotomy is another truth: a lot of homegrown religion presently wreaks havoc within the church. It does appear that there is an unusual connection between the church house and our house.

The connection is unusual, not because of its deviant abnormalities. The connection is unusual in that it is too often ignored, or goes unnoticed. Too often we choose to ignore the fact that there is a connection, a bridge, a relationship, an association between the church family and our family. The household of God is essentially made out of the households men and women. There is a link between the behavior within the church house and the behavior patterns in our house.

Jesus' first act of healing took place within the synagogue, or the church house. There, within the church as a part of the normal crowd was a man filled with demons. The man was no stranger to the religious gathering. His aberrant behavior was seemingly common and acceptable. The congregation had grown accustomed to his frequent outbursts. He was a permanent fixture among the membership.

Jesus freed the man from his demon-possessed lifestyle. Through the power of preaching and sound teaching, unclean spirits were silenced and sent running. Jesus, within the church, did what no other power could do.

However, as I continued reading Mark's witness, I noticed something deeply disturbing. I noticed that Jesus immediately left the church house and went to Simon and Andrew's house. The Bible says, "And immediately he left the synagogue, and entered the house of Simon and Andrew." Within the house was a woman, Simon's mother-in-law, sick with fever. In one sentence, Jesus moves from the church house to Simon's house; from a demon-filled man to a fever-filled woman. It does not take much imagination to suggest that Jesus recognized the connection between aberrant behavior in the church house and conditions in Simon's house. This unusual connection is traced by our Lord.

It is rather interesting that educators, psychologists, psychiatrists, and other behavioral scientists begin their search of aberrant behavior with an inquiry of personal history. Personal history always begins at home. The inquiry of one's home environment provides invaluable clues to abnormal and destructive behavior patterns. A student who disturbs the class, or demonstrates personal suffering, is usually asked about home. What's going on at home is the lead-off question to a child whose studies have deteriorated. A man, or woman, who once eagerly smiled but now has a frown etched grotesquely upon his/her face, prompts the concerned to wonder about his/her home.

It is rather unusual that the church, as a whole, chooses to ignore the church-home connection. It is rather strange because the people within the church house live in some other house. In fact, they live in the other house more than they live in the church house. They do more things in their house than they do in the church house. People are more human in the living house than they are in the church house. Pastors give more attention to the things that affect people in their living house than they do with matters of the church house. The church ought to see that if behavior is strange or destructive in the church house, then something is strangely destroying them in the living house.

Sociologists of religion claim that persons unable to sustain happy, fruitful, and healthy relationships at home are prime candidates for "hell raisers" at the church. Persons, who are uncommitted and unstable in relationships, are often uncommitted and unstable in their relationship with the Lord. Individuals who have never come to trust, love, understand, and care for another bring their distrust, suspicions, and hurts to the church. Children, who are abused and misused at home, usually discover either a positive or negative outlet at the church. It is also held that persons who maintain and sustain happy, healthy, fruitful, and committed relationships at home are better workers, worshipers, and neighbors.

Now Mark's testimony is not specific, but it is most implicit that Jesus recognized a connection between the demon-filled man at the church and the fever-filled woman in Simon's house. The healing of the man in the synagogue prompts Jesus to immediately go to Simon's house. It could be argued that the man was using the church house, not to worship God; but as a get away from his wife. Maybe the man wanted to faithfully serve the Lord, but his wife hindered him by casting evil spells. Maybe she constantly challenged his manhood, thus robbing him of his dignity. Maybe he made her unhappy, so she reciprocated and made him unhappy.

I know of numerous situations where fever in a home caused demons in the church. A home hot with hell produces individuals who can surely raise hell. The decadence of our world—crime, drugs, AIDS, wars, terrorism, and sadism are the immediate results of a breakdown in our homes. Homelessness is not the result of no house, it's the result of no home, no situation where relationships are revered and respected.

We are living in a time where hardly anything surprises us. A man will kill his mother, rape his grandmother, addict his sister, and rob his father. Things that were once considered unbelievable have become common news. The Bible speaks of the day when "the children's teeth are set on edge because of the sour grapes eaten by the fathers." Yes, our world, even the church, has become a bastion of the demonic because of the fevers of anxiety, fear, restlessness, self-seeking, greed, and lust that wreck our homes. Redd Foxx once said, "Find an ugly child and follow him [her] home and see who answers the door." Follow some of these ugly acting, demon-filled church folk home, and see what kind of pain-filled, lonely, and loveless situations await them.

Jesus understood the connection. He understands it, even now. It is rather hard to serve Jesus, when your spirit is torn apart by a ripped apart home. Jesus knows it is rather difficult to sing Zion songs, when the "blues" await you at home. He knows church praying is painful, when prayers are unanswered at home. Jesus knows of the artificiality of church membership, when there is no supporting relationship at home. He knows the preacher's sermons can be painfully hollow, when there is nothing but a shell at home. He knows we are more prone to issue forth cutting words, when no kind words are heard at home. Jesus knows our deeds are likely to be damnable, when no goodness meets us at home. Jesus knows about this unusual connection, so He does not stay at the church house—He comes to my house. He comes to your house.

The Bible says, " Jesus entered the house and they told Him about the fever-filled woman." Brothers and Sisters, if the home situation is filled with a fever—tell the Lord about it. Yet make sure that Jesus is there because you brought Him there. Make certain that the Jesus of worship lives with you, as the Jesus of practice. And if you bring Him home, in your life, tell Him all about the problem. If drugs are destroying someone in your house, as they are in mine, please join me in telling Jesus all about it. If distrust and dishonesty is wrecking your home, tell the Lord all about it. If some evil force is killing your family, tell the Lord about it. The Lord is interested in the fevers in our homes.

When they informed Jesus of the fever-filled woman, the Lord went and "took her by the hand and lifted her up." The story is "the fever left her." Jesus gave the woman what she needed. The fever-filled woman needed to be lifted up.

We can do more good in relationships, if we quit putting people down and start lifting them up. The truth is no one can put us down as viciously as one's family. Jesus is not a Savior who puts people down. He comes to lift us up. If your marriage is going down, He can lift it up. If children are going down, He can lift them up. And children, if parents are going down, Jesus can lift up mother and He can lift up father. Once Jesus lifts them up, the fever will surely leave.

Notice how Jesus blesses the unusual connection. As soon as the fever left the woman, the Bible says, she served them. When the fever had gone out, she busied herself in faithful service. As soon as the problem was corrected, she gave of herself in the service of the Lord. As soon as the house became a home, she became more useful than she had previously been. It is worthy of note that the man at church praised Him, whereas, the woman at home served Him.

I appreciate persons who serve the Lord because they know the Lord lifted them up. I thank God for people, who once they were healed, start faithfully serving the Lord.

I lift up in glorious honor all who are sensible and thankful enough to serve Him who saved them. Brothers and Sisters, no one can really serve the Lord until they have been lifted up. Moreover, a lifted up home makes for a lifted up church. A healed home makes for a healed church. A healed sinner makes for a helpful saint. A lot of church folk cannot serve and will not serve because they have not been healed.

Jesus stands as the link between the power of God in the church house, and the needs of broken humanity in the living-house. If God touches you in the church house, then God can lift you up when you go home.

If it means anything, I can testify as to what happens when Jesus lifts you up. There was once a fever in the relationship between me and my father. I thought Daddy was mean and unreasonable. Thus, I fled from everything Daddy stood for. I left the church, dropped out of school, forsook the straight and narrow way. But one day the Lord lifted me up, turned me around, and the fever of parental resentment left me and I began to serve the Lord. Now I hold Daddy up in great esteem. I worship the ground he walks upon.

I once did not respect the sisters. I used them and abused them. But one day the Lord lifted me up, and the fever of disrespect left me. Now, I love the sisters. I promote the queenliness of the Black woman.

I once did not really trust the brethren. I believed that every brother was trying to "get over" on me. I suspected every brother as an enemy. But Jesus came into my life, lifted me up, and spoke, "You know when you pass from darkness to light, when you love the brethren." Now I can stand, today, and honestly say, "the fever has left me. I love the brethren, respect the sisters, adore the children, and treasure the elderly. The Lord lifted me up!

REVIVAL IN THE HOME

Text: *"And they came to Jesus, and saw the demoniac sitting there, clothed in his right mind, the man who had the legion; and they were afraid. And those who had seen it told what had happened to the demoniac and to the swine. And they began to beg Jesus to depart from their neighborhood. And as he was getting into the boat, the man who had been possessed with demons begged him that he might be with him. But he refused, and said to him, 'Go home to your friends, and tell them how much the Lord has done for you, and how he has had mercy on you.' And he went away and began to proclaim in the Decapolis how much Jesus had done for him; and all men marveled"* (***Mark 5:15-20, RSV***).

Our preacher, Reverend C. E. McLain, who highlighted our Fall Revival for five years, shared with me an experience from the pages of his pastoral ministry. As we were sharing a meal, he told me of an incident in his ministry that had the potential to be most volatile. During a significant moment in his ministry, a certain church officer disappointed him and frustrated the progress of the church in a disturbing way. Reverend McLain confessed that the actions of the officer infuriated him, incensed him so, that he had to grab the edge of his desk before he lost control. Such behavior was so uncharacteristic of McLain, that he concluded that his "ancestors" must have taken hold of him. His advice to me, from the lesson of that experience, was "to know your ancestors." Acquaint yourself with the powerful spirits of those who make you what you are. Carlyle Marney admonished us to "bless your roots"; bless them by understanding them.

Upon reading the story of the man of Gadarene, I was captured by some disturbing truths that refused to let me go. One of those truths which I believe ought to be announced early as today is too many folk go through life not really knowing where they live. Too many of us do not know the emotional, spiritual, psychological, and social addresses of our ancestors. In essence, we fail to realize what makes us what we are. The identifiable formations of what makes us act the way we do often escapes us.

The story of the Gadarene man calls attention to the fact that we can be lost in our own world. While the man was out of control, the text says, "he dwelt, (he lived) among the tombstones." He made the community graveyard his home. His address was the cemetery. The forces that interfered with him becoming a whole person informed him that his rent was being paid among the dead, and that tombstones made excellent pillows.

I recently heard a preacher note that we are organized for death. Think about it! It did not take America a week to fill the deserts of Saudi Arabia, and the waters of the Persian Gulf, with instruments of destruction and men and women armed to kill. There is something tragically awful about the mental and spiritual dynamics of this present age, which finds most of us getting active around death-ushering realities. Many of our families never get together until some tragedy, death, or a funeral. Many of our congregations/church houses never fill up until there is either a fight or a funeral. We are organized for death!

The man lived within the graveyard, among the dead. His whole life was organized around death. When the society tried to place him under control, he also refused to live where the society wanted him to live. I grew up during the sixties. I graduated in the last year of the sixties, 1969. The sixties were a time of great protest and social upheaval. The world changed during the sixties and has never been the same again. In parts of the East and West coast, the Black church almost went about of business. In fact, the church has never recovered from the turbulence of the sixties. As I now ponder the bristling activities of that infamous time, I hear more clearly what the protest was all about. We were essentially saying to a death loving culture, "we refuse to live where you want us to live. We refuse to live under the emotional, psychological, spiritual, and social shackles and chains. We refuse to live under the control of racial and sexual designations. We were not accepting the inhuman addresses that an insensitive society was assigning us. Even if it took hurting ourselves, we were not going to exist within the dehumanizing boundaries of a culture that does not even know its own address."

When Jesus delivered the man from his death-dealing situation, Jesus ordered the man to "go home." Once the man was clothed in his right mind, Jesus commissioned the man to "go home." I am rallied by the suggestions within the Lord's command. I hear something, which I believe offers us life in spite of a death-dealing society. Jesus points the man where we all should be pointed if we are to fully apprehend the resurrection faith. To a man whose address was the graveyard, Jesus commissioned the man to return to his home.

Someone has said that "we are not bad people wanting to be good, we are sick people trying to get well." The Psalmist declared that we are "born in sin and shaped in iniquity." I want to posit, in this sermon, that most of our struggles, weaknesses, negativities, inadequacies, and even our sicknesses are home-bred. The problems that globally plague our world are homemade. The demons that hurl us, hurt us, and haunt us are home-bred, home-fed demons. I want to also posit that for us to be fully well, we will have to return home. When I speak of home, I refer not to a place, a city, nor a state, nor even a country. I refer to what C. E. McClain suggested —a thorough and exacting confrontation with our ancestors. I refer us to an honest examination, a realistic inquiry of the behavior patterns, lifestyles, thinking, values, notable strengths, and glaring shortcomings of our ancestors, of our family tree.

One of the painful realities which we often choose to ignore is that our parents were not as perfect as we paint them. Our dear ol' Dads and Moms were also "born in sin and shaped in iniquity." They, too, "fell short of the glory of God." They, too, "missed the mark." They, too, needed Jesus. They, too, needed a Savior, who could deliver them from the demons of this world. They, too, were a part of a world that breeds persons to deny crucial realities about life and living. Unfortunately, they, too, were often dishonest about dealing with who they were and how they got in their respective conditions.

Anne Wilson-Shaef in her moving treatment, <u>When Society Becomes An Addict</u>, notes the three "ifs" of the addict. The three "ifs" of the addict are: "if only, as if, and what if." The "if only" addict is being dishonest about the past. The "as if " addict is being dishonest about the present. The "what if " addict is dishonest about the future. I want to jump within the middle of these addicted "ifs," and highlight the "as if " addict, those who are being dishonest about the present. "As if " folk are out of touch with the way things are. They are like actors perpetually in character. "As if " people never want to risk learning the truth. They never want to test relationships. They never want to experience the truth of family.

The Gadarene man could have been an "as if " personality. He lived among tombs "as if " that was where he was supposed to live. He acted out a character "as if " that was who he really was. He hurt himself "as if " that was what he was supposed to do. He made a lot of eerie and unnecessary noise "as if " such noise was normal for him. The story adds "he was brought under chains." Society tried to control him "as if " that was the right thing to do. Society tried to control his energy "as if " they knew what was best for the man. Society tried to break his spirit "as if " he needed them to do for him what he seemingly could not do for himself.

Most of us live out life the way we do "as if" that is the way life is supposed to be. We have taken our home-bred, home-fed, home-grown demons into the world "as if" they generate the expected norms. We relate to the world, to one another, even to God, "as if" we are normal and every-thing is all right. Most folk, particularly black folk, use religion as an escape rather than to face our true selves. We mainly want to "feel good," "as if" feeling good will make us be good and make us completely whole. As I wrestled with this text, I struggled to see how I might preach all that text was suggesting in one sermon. Dishonesty infected my sermon preparation, "as if" one sermon could adequately reveal all that the text was revealing.

Jesus told the man to "go home." The man wanted to follow Jesus "as if" salvation was exclusively devotion. He wanted to develop another "as if" syndrome and lose himself afresh in religious escape. Some of the most lost folk I know are in church. They do not know who they really are and use religion to deny what actually is. The psychic contagion of entire congregations tempts churches to go through business-as-usual "as if" business is usual. The time comes in all of our lives when we must "go home."

Jesus does not save us from one illusion to give us an-other illusion. The Lord wants us to be real, real with Him and our world. We can never be totally free of the demons that would wreck our lives if we never go back home. No-tice, the man could in no way free himself. He could not deliver himself from his destructive ways. Dishonesty is always destructive. The society could not control the man, and I don't believe that society wanted him free. The text suggests that the society was more content with a demon-crazed man than they were with him sane, and with a demon-chasing Savior at his side. In a sin-shaped, death-dealing society freedom is never on the agenda. Control is the name of the game. If we cannot control human beings, we rather not have anything to do with them.

Most of us have been raised by control mechanisms. Our homes were bastions of control. Family relationships were relationships of control. Someone was always pulling switches and levers of control. If it wasn't a father with a loud voice, cussing and fussing; it was a mother yelling and screaming. If it wasn't a father controlling with his earnings, it was a mother controlling with her influence. Husbands try to control wives by withholding certain comforts. Wife tries to control husband by withholding spousal affections. Parents work long and hard, sacrifice and suffer, all in the name of control. Parents are more into control than they are into love, as evidenced in the many outbursts of " I feed you and house you. Therefore, you must do as I say." Parents use control mechanisms, rather than love's message. I have seen parents who were drunks/addicts, who control the family through their addictions. Children internalize such behavior "as if " it is normal. It comes off as normal to them because they don't know any better.

We enter into a world that tells us to "work hard"—control. We are educated to work hard rather than work smart. The church tells us to be nice—control. The law tells us to be good—control. The constitution tells us to be loyal—control. The strategy has not changed from the days of the Gadarene man. Society wants to control us, more than set us free.

Society tried to put chains on the man, but he broke them and pulled them apart. He broke society's compulsions and pulled things apart. Unfortunately, he pulled family apart. He pulled marital relations apart. He pulled community apart. What else could a man who was out of control do, but break up and pull apart? People out of control usually specialize in breaking up and pulling things apart. When we are out of control, we break up our homes and pull apart meaningful relationships.

However, Jesus came into the man's life. Jesus, the

integrator of personality. Jesus, the liberator of personhood. Jesus, the reconciler of full humanity. Jesus, the one who fixes what is broken up and puts back together what has been pulled apart. Under the influence of Jesus, the man was put in his right mind. He was delivered from other minds and put in his right mind. He was rescued from the wrong mind and placed in his right mind. Society no longer had control of his mind; he had his own mind.

Our world can only be redeemed when we, Black Christians, begin to think for ourselves. Church life becomes more meaningful when people are rescued from the herd, and start thinking for themselves. Every congregation needs some disciples who have been placed in their right mind. Our families will only be saved, when we start thinking for ourselves. Our young people will become whole people when they use their right minds. If we are to be organized for life, rather than death, we must be clothed and in our right minds.

Of interest, again, is what Jesus tells the man. The man wanted only to be with Jesus. He wanted nothing more than to follow Jesus, but Jesus told the man to "go home." A proper return home must come by Jesus, for only God can put us in our right minds. Only God can deliver us from this death-dealing, control-oriented mind. Only God can deliver us from the home-bred, home-fed, home-grown demons that dwarf and demonize our humanity. However, it should be noted that God does not save us for mere religious devotion. God saves us for responsible duty. And the first duty we have for God and humanity is to "go home." The redeemed remnant of the Black family has the responsibility of going home to the ghettoes of our upbringing. We have the responsibility of going to the urban jungles of our humble beginnings. The Lord is telling us, "Go home to those who made us what we are and tell them that God has remade us into what we should be. Tell them what great things the Lord has done for us."

Tell them how God has had mercy upon us.
Tell them how God has quenched our thirst.
Tell them how God has satisfied our hunger.
Tell them how God has removed our shame.
Tell them how God has cured us of trouble.
Tell them how God has returned our loss.
Tell them how God has calmed our turmoil.
Tell them how God has paid our debt.
Tell them how God has freed our souls.

GOD'S MARRIAGE PROCESS

Text: *"Then the man said, 'This at last is bone of my bones and flesh of my flesh; she shall be called Woman, because she was taken out of Man.' Therefore a man leaves his father and his mother and cleaves to his wife, and they become one flesh. And the man and his wife were both naked, and were not ashamed." (Genesis 2:23-25,* RSV)*

Someone has accurately stated that "the downfall of a civilization begins in the family." Such a statement is most sobering, solemn, and serious, particularly when we gaze upon the landscape of the Black family. It has become common knowledge that over fifty percent of all Black families are being led by single, young, and often illiterate and underemployed women. Some years ago Daniel Moynihan reported that the Black family was primarily matriarchal. The female led Black family was viewed as the seed bed for family instability within the Black community. Moynihan's report could certainly be challenged. There is, indeed, some exceptional parenting being done in single-parent homes. A lot of women are doing a superb job in holding together the Black family structure. Yet, the truth is the Black family is not doing so good.

The diminishing health of the Black family centers around that which is fundamental to family life—the marriage of men and women. It appears that we are having a painfully tough, and often futile time with marriage. Marriage, for all practical purposes, is the foundation of family life. Incidently, it is with marital life that we are taking a terrible beating. It is not with single-parenting. It is with men and women withholding their vows to marital commitment. Statistics reveal that over one-third of all Black marriages end in divorce. One out of every three couples who walk down these aisles may well walk in vain and in pain. It appears that we are specializing in weddings, but flunking out on marriages. I heard my great-uncle once say, "There are a whole lot of men with the wrong wife, and a lot of women with the wrong husband." We may not all agree with his marital assessment, but it just seems difficult for us to stay together.

I was recently riding with one of our associate ministers and in a rare instance the radio was playing. A particular song captured our attention. Al Green was singing, "Let's Stay Together." The song that followed "Let's Stay Together" was also by Al Green. This song, however, was "How Can You Mend A Broken Heart?" Turn on the radio! Listen to our love lyrics! Inevitably we will catch some sister singing, "Caught up in the rapture of your love." An oldie but goodie may find some brother announcing a "Mighty Love." But with all of the love oozing out of our songs, we are having a difficult time making marriages work.

I recently heard a man ask: " Is it more uncomfortable to be single and wish you were married? Or, to be married and wish you were not?" What's happening to our marriages? Did God make a grand error when He instituted marriage? Or, do we not understand what marriage is all about? I dare to contend that we have yet to fully embrace God's marriage process. We have yet to see God's intention, God's purpose, God's will for marriage.

I believe that even our children know that marriage is not made out of love songs. When was the last time a love song put a broken marriage back together? Allow me to serve notice, this morning, that weddings will not be foolishly adorned with romance songs during marriage ceremonies at the Olivet Church! If that is what you want to do, go downtown and let the justice of peace marry you. (It appears that is where most of us end up anyway.) God has a plan for marriage and I believe God's plan is the best plan. I claim no marriage perfection. I cannot even claim immunity to marital destruction. My own parents divorced after being married for over twenty years. My wife's parents divorced. Statistically, we are headed to the divorce court. Our marriage is not even supposed to make it. However, I believe in God. I still believe that "what God has joined together, let no man (or woman) put asunder."

Listen to this ancient text! There in the first book of the Bible is an existential synopsis of what marriage is all about. In a few short sentences, marriage's eternal purpose is announced. The creation story moved to its close and God makes the announcement: "it is not good for man to live alone." Humanity needed a helpmate, not a god, nor a creature. God perceived a need for a "Helpmate." As mysteriously as God created the man, God also created the woman. Brethren, no male-human can take credit for the creation of woman by claiming in the buffoonery of Archie Bunker, "she came from my rib." If you Brothers check your ribs, you will discover that all of your ribs are still there. Not one of us is a rib short.

The truth of this text is that the man knows nothing about where the woman comes from. God has placed him in a deep sleep. He is literally dead to the world, ignorant of the mighty acts of God. God created [hu]man, male and female, man and woman. "Man and woman are the gift of God to one another." When the brother awakened, he beheld God's gift and proclaimed, "This at last is bone of my bones and flesh of my flesh...." Allow me to say it like the Brothers might say it, "Wow, this is what I've been waiting for. This is the real deal. Here is a part of me! In fact, the woman makes me a better, more wholesome, complete person."

One of the great tragedies of marriages is that many

never move beyond the "beholding perspective." The "beholding perspective" has been the point of much perversion and abuse. Too many brothers see the sisters as just bone of bone and flesh of flesh. Women are perceived as sexual toys, something that looks good and feels good. I once thought only we, the brothers, were so shallow in relationships. I thought it was only the brothers who sat around and shared their sexual exploits. Ironically, the sisters have also joined the sexual olympics and are winning gold medals. " Bone of my bone and flesh of my flesh."

God's purpose for marriage is not just bones and flesh. The real goal is for two people to join in spiritual companionship, not physical exploitation. A marriage is dead on arrival that attempts to live only for bones of one's bones and flesh of one's flesh, for people are more than bones and flesh. God created human beings. God breathed a part of God's self and "[hu]man became a living soul." Let us be mindful that a part of God lives in every foxy sister and every "hunk" brother. People are better appreciated when viewed as spiritual beings, spiritual equals, and not just bones and flesh.

Again, this ancient text says more about marriage than all the love songs written and sung. Marriage, blessed of God, is a process. To be in process signifies being produced. The word "process" means a "system of operations that produce something." Marriage is a system of operations that produces something, and not just babies. Marriages produce wholesome, healthy, and happy people. A marriage is the production point of fulfilled and fruitful people. Marriages die when they cease to be in process; when the operations cease; when the goals of productions are not clearly defined. The truth is when God's ultimate objectives no longer energize the motors of marital relationships production ceases.

Verse 25 gives us the process of God's marriage. In a one line marriage ceremony, the process is stated. "Therefore a man leaves his father and mother and cleaves to his wife, and they become one flesh." The verbs of the text describe the process. The first step in the marital operation is to leave. "When a man leaves...." Inasmuch as the text says man, it includes woman. However, the emphasis on <u>man</u> needs to be explained. The point that the text emphasizes is a mature person, a man/woman; and not a boy, or a girl. Maturity of person is a valid prerequisite for an enduring marriage. Marriage is not a plaything to be experimented with because of youthful urges and childish passions.

The records reveal that youthful marriage is precarious at best. A young person, not quite out of adolescence, rarely makes an ideal candidate for marriage. Young people need to first know who they are, understand enough about themselves, have a sense of personal goals, as well as a sense of what they want out of life before inviting another into their lives. Simply put, we must own enough of ourselves before we can adequately share ourselves with somebody else. Youthful marriages are very difficult, particularly, when it comes down to leaving the homes of Mom and Dad. We have painfully discovered that "shot-gun weddings" kill all concerned. It is tragic to force people into a marriage because of some youthful mistakes.

How in the world can a boy treat a woman right, when he hasn't even learned how to treat himself right? How in the world can a girl understand the commitment of marriage, when all she has experienced is "puppy love?" Yet, the big problem plaguing kids-in-marriage is the problem of leaving.

The biblical text calls for maturity in marriage. Marriage calls for a level of maturity that facilitates leaving the comforts of home and accepting the challenges of marital commitment. It is the transference of responsible relationships. It is commonly noted that in-laws have hurt many marriages; but the text is not focusing exclusively on in-laws. It is a call for a mature person to leave the circle of self and take a journey with another. It is a call for maturity, to put away with childish things and infantile behavior. It is a call to put away the comfortable ideas of one's own family and create a new family, heretofore not known.

Too many of us are guilty of trying to make our families carbon copies of our parents. We must leave and let God do a new thing in our marriage. Each marriage must journey to God on its own level of faith, with only the foundational assistance of our parental upbringing.

There are also many who want to push childhood fantasies and fairy tale notions upon the family. "We're going to live happily ever after," many assume. We must leave such childish fantasies because each marriage represents two unique individuals, never before married to one another; who are writing a new story, firmly rooted in reality. Thus, the first step in God's marriage process is "to leave."

The second step is "cleave to" one's spouse. A lot of brothers and sisters have missed this step. "Cleave to" does not mean to glue yourself to the sister's petticoat, not giving her room to breathe nor yourself room to grow. Such cleaving smothers individuality. "Cleave to" does not mean beating someone into your way of thinking, doing, acting and reacting. Everyone is born with his/her own head, own brain, and own God-given inclinations. "Cleaving to" doesn't mean butchering to pieces.

Just as "to leave" suggests mobilizing maturity; "cleave to" suggests engaging commitment. Too many Black male/female relationships, marriages in particular, lie littered on the ash heaps of non-commitment. Family life goes no-where once wrecked by non-commitment. Commitment is more than lip-service to a relationship. Commitment is whole-life orientation, an orienting of one's life away from one's self. A definition of commitment is "the decision to actively eliminate options." Too many of us want to live in relationships with a variety of options. A lot of options in relationships equal no commitment.

If a marriage is to be in process, as God intends, options must be eliminated. The voice of many options speaks on this wise: "I don't have to put up with this, I can do something different. I don't need you, I can make it by myself (or find somebody else). My life was different, even better, before I married you." Too many options!

Commitment is best expressed within an atmosphere of sensitivity. "Cleaving to" is not cutting down. Insensitivity within a family is like running a car with no oil, cooking food without moisture, skating on gravel, or riding a bike in sand. It's difficult! It's cruel! It's messy! It's mean! It's a grinding task, an unbearable feat; it is humanly impossible.

Marriages demand that husbands and wives be committed enough to be sensitive to one another. We must never try to mold God's creation into our image and likeness. We must become so united that the welfare of the other becomes vitally important. Both individuals must grow, flourish, and blossom. When a flower withers, or a leaf dries up, detachment from the plant is inevitable. No few marriages are withering, drying up because of an unfulfilled wife, or a dissatisfied husband. The passage where Paul writes, "Wives submit to your husbands and husbands submit to your wives" could best read: "be sensitive to one another." What is important to one person's needs must be respected by the other. Just because my wife does not have a passion for fishing does not mean I need to stop fishing. Our vows did read "Through better or for worse, sickness or in health, richer or poorer"—cleave to one another!

Yes, first we must leave. Secondly, we must cleave. One leaves only to cleave. Finally, "they become one flesh." Notice, they do not short one another out. The two remain, as individuals, distinct in form and flavor. Yet, the two with different tastes, different backgrounds, different parents, different ideas, different careers, different sex, different body shapes, become one functioning entity in the service of God. Dietrich Bonhoeffer once said, in response to this text, "they were one from their origin and only when they become one do they return to their origin." In other words, man and woman come from one God and only as they become one with each other do they return to God.

The great testimony of a marriage in process is when two different individuals start looking alike. (We all know persons who have been married so long that they start looking alike.) They not only look alike, but they seem to be traveling in the same direction. What we are witnessing is a marriage that has stood the test of time, endured trials, and withstood tribulations. Two became one when each dared to leave and decided to cleave. Through the good times, as well as the bad times they decided to cleave. When days were difficult, no one threw up his/her hands, called it quits and walked out on the other. When pains were deep, wounds ugly, hurts unbearable—they stayed committed and trusted in God. Someone in the marriage understood God's purpose and they both embraced God's marriage process.

To become one flesh, husbands and wives must believe that the same Mystery that brings us together can keep us together. To become one flesh is to accept God's process in marriage. God's marriage process finds us being hammered with humility, forged in forgiveness, grounded in selflessness, nurtured in understanding, pressed with patience, seasoned in suffering, and polished by God's grace.

No wonder Christ likened the church to a bride. "A marriage is the church in original form." And like the church, a marriage needs the Lord. God made us. God knows us. God cares for us and with God our marriages can survive. With God, our families will thrive; with God, we can leave, cleave, and become one. With God, bills can be paid. With God, children can be raised. With God, all things are possible.

Brothers and Sisters, don't allow your marriage to crash. Please don't stop your marriage. Keep the marriage train in motion. It's a good journey that leads "all the way from earth to heaven."

God cares!
God Cares!
God cares!

THE FAMILY IS FOR THE CHILDREN

Text: *"Unless the Lord builds the house, those who build it labor in vain. Unless the Lord watches over the city, the watch-man stays awake in vain. It is in vain that you rise up early and go late to rest, eating the bread of anxious toil; for he gives to his beloved sleep. Lo, sons are a heritage from the Lord, the fruit of the womb a reward. Like arrows in the hand of a war-rior are the sons of one's youth. Happy is the man who has his quiver full of them. He shall not be put to shame when he speaks with his enemies in the gate."* (**Psalm 127**, Revised Standard Version)

Among the many startling realities revealed in the Bible is the frailty of humanity. God's crown creation, the one lower than angels, always falls short. The Bible's pages are full of people like you and me, which means the Bible has no saints. It has some fairly decent people, but none comes off so virtuous as to claim sainthood. Even the Bible's family structures are filled with negative inadequa-cies. There is brother against brother, Cain and Abel; brother against sister; a son against father, David and Absalom; mothers showing favoritism, Rebekah and Jacob; fathers having special sons, Jacob and Joseph; sibling ri-valries, Joseph and his brothers; incest, in Sodom and Gomorra; adultery, fornication, even a brother raping a sister. The Bible's families are so much like yours and mine, always missing the mark of divine intention.

I believe it is time for someone to raise the question: When God delivered the people out of Egypt, why didn't God just give them the Promised Land without all of the wilderness stuff? The God, mostly made in our image, would not have included the tough times of the wilderness with the business of redemption. Why all of the water from rocks, serpents, bread from heaven, fire by night, clouds by day, smoke around the mountains, and laws etched in stone? Yet, Egypt to the Promised Land never comes without first going through the wilderness.

Redemption is always from Egypt, through the wilderness, and then on to the Promised Land. Our blessings never come without trials, without struggles, without sacrifices. The wilderness is God's way of chiseling human effort in harmony with divine purpose. It happened to Jesus, and it happens to me and you.

The reason God gives us the wilderness is to keep our faith in perspective. The wilderness hammers in the awesome fact that the Promised Land is never ours—it is for our children. On the other side of our wildernesses awaits a Promised Land for our children. Our struggles equal our children's strength. Our sacrifices equal our children's successes. Our pain equals our children's gain. Our crosses equal our children's crown.

In America the family presently lives in a wilderness. People are getting married at record rates. Yet, most of those getting married have walked down the aisles once before. Over fifty percent of those recently married are marrying for the second time. In other words, people divorce as often as they marry.

Black families are in the most precarious position since slavery. Over fifty percent of our households are led by single parents. Most of our children are born in poverty. Young black men fill the jails and armed forces in disproportionate numbers. A young black male has a greater chance of being killed, imprisoned, or probationed than he has of getting a college degree and a decent job. The sociological formula for a full prison scholarship is often: single parent + no positive male image + high school dropout = a convict.

We have a line in our prayers, "Lord, I didn't bow for shape, form, or fashion." I wish our families would have applied that line to our family configurations. Most of our homes, particularly our marriages, are overwhelmingly concerned about shape, form, and fashion. A lot of unhappy people are living out family life for shape, form, and fashion. The shape describes how we became family. The form identifies who is the family. (A lot of people are married to the "who", the form of marriage.) Then many are guilty of the fashion of family, the why we became family. However, not many of us consider the function of family.

Shape, form, and fashion answer how, who, and why. Function deals with "what." The function of, the "what" of the family is greater than how, who, and why, and certainly more meaningful. The "what" of family empowers us to live within the wilderness, in hope of the Promised Land.

In a startling book entitled, <u>The Family Crucible</u>, it is suggested that the "lack of adequate structure within a family is a larger cause of family pain and dysfunction." The personality disorders, attitudinal misshapes, inadequate world-views, and low opinions of ourselves are often the direct results of our families. Our families may have done the best they knew to do, but that does not dismiss the fact of their many failures. Most of us are subject to die in the family wilderness, because we have failed to see who the family is for. The family, as God intends, is for the children.

There is nothing in the Bible that suggests the family being for the benefit of a bride and groom. Bride and groom may receive some satisfaction out of the family arrangement, but the family is not for them. Even in single-parent situations, the family is still for the children. Even where there are no biological children, God ordained family structure to be a blessing for the children. Parental blessing is the result of children being blessed. Children determine parenthood, not vice-versa.

Think about it! A car is not created for itself. A car

can never function as a self-determined, self-fulfilling creation. A house is not built for self-service, unless it is a haunted house. (Maybe that is why so many families are filled with haunts?) As remarkable an instrument as the computer is, the computer is not built for itself. The car, the house, the computer, even this world, are instruments and realities that exist only to serve others. All are utilitarian in purpose. Delight in something has to do with proper use.

So it is with the family. The family serves as an intergenerational vehicle. We are all the children of a family. Our families serve best when understood best. The family represents God's vessel for transporting the truths of faith from children to children to children. "So when your children pass this way and ask what mean these stones," puts this truth in the context of family. Likewise, "The fathers eat the sour grapes, but the children's teeth are set on edge." The failure of the family to function as God intends has horrendous consequences on our children. Unhappiness is basically the result of misuse.

The truth can be quite painful, but if the family is not for the children it is against the children. Even as I speak, the selfishness of our culture has worked against the children. The recklessness of teenage parenting is against the children. Mothers and fathers living in separate homes is against our children. Although no one should remain married when marital discord is harming children, divorce is against the children. Child abuse is against our children. Babies having babies is against our children.

Our nation has incurred a debt of mammoth proportion. Right now we are passing on to our children an unpaid bill in the trillions. The war madness of our world destroys children, however patriotic it might make us feel. Racism is against families; therefore, it is against our children. Pollution and toxic waste are against our children.

Whatever is not for our children is against our children. The church which seeks to pamper selfish adults and worship the days past and gone is against our children. Wherever there is a congregation not helping families, not seeking the welfare of the young, not investing in its children—there is a congregation that is against children.

We are no better than the despots of China, who in the eyes of the world, turned guns on its children in Tiannamen Square. If we are not for the children, we are against the children.

Psalm 127 lifts before us the blessed effects of viewing the family for the children. The challenge of this text can bless us all. Allow me to briefly cite three calls that I hear coming from the psalmist. The first call is a call to consider God. Verse one says, "Unless the Lord builds the house they labor in vain who build it; unless the Lord watches the city, the watchman awakes in vain."

The family is of God. God calls us into relationship. It was God's wisdom that saw that it was not good for us to live alone. Whatever our family configuration, God allowed it to be so. God gives us life. All life comes from God. It does not matter how smart we are; what plans we contrive; the amount of our money; who we know, or where we think we are going—unless God works through us, we are working in vain.

A family is blessed that always considers God. Such a reality does not mean that a family will not have problems; that the children will all turn out right; that conflicts will be eliminated; or that the bills will be paid on time. Families are problem-prone. Healthy families, however, live through problems; whereas, unhealthy families are destroyed by problems.

Then there are some problems that only God can solve. God has to be recognized as the ultimate problem solver. Consider God as the One who ultimately builds the family.

Consider God, who can build up families that have been torn down. Consider God as the One who watches over families better than guns, bombs, bullets, or big bank accounts. Consider God who holds tomorrow and who cares about the tomorrows which will hold our children.

Secondly, I hear God's call into fruitful labor for our families. Verse 2 brings to our attention the futility of our labor, when God is not considered. The psalmist lets us know that it's "vain for you to rise up early, to sit up late, to eat the bread of sorrow." A common phrase among today's parents is, "I'm trying to make life easier for my children." If God does not make it easier for our children, we labor in vain.

We can work all the jobs we can find. We can get up as early as we like. We can stay up all night working, or worrying. Yet, until God's vision of the family breaks in upon us, we labor in vain. When family is viewed as for the children, we may quit some of our jobs and quit staying awake so late. Our children need us more than we need all of our jobs. If we gave our children more of us and less of the material what-nots of vain-filled labor, our children would be much better. I need to spend more time with mine and you with yours. I might not always be the pastor of a church, but I will always have my children. Mothers and Fathers who view the family as God does understand fruitful labor does not mean endless labor. The best fruit we can give to this world is the labor invested in children. Church! You can truly be blest by laboring with our children.

Thirdly, God calls us to experience true happiness by understanding family as being for the children. I stated earlier the folly of many who stay married only for the sake of the children. Allow me to footnote that assertion by adding until you rediscover some other reason to stay married, the children represent a good one. Again, the family is for the children. Only God gives us children. God did not have to do it, but He did.

The Psalmist says, "Behold, children are a heritage of the Lord." It then says, "Happy is the man who has his quiver full of them." The imagery used is that of an archer aiming at a target. The quiver is the sack on his back used to hold arrows. The arrows are used by the archer to hit the target. The archer's joy is hitting the target. The arrows are not the archer, but they represent the archer.

Brothers and Sisters, God has blessed us with families. Our families are like the quiver on an archer's back. God has also filled our families/quivers with children. Our children are not us, although they represent us. God allows us to experience happiness when our children hit the mark. However, they can never reach the mark without our aiming them. That is why the wise say, "Train up a child in the way he should go and when he grows old he will not stray away." It does not say, "Train the child the way you think he should go," or "they think he should go"; but in the way God wants him/her to go. In other words, aim children at God's target. If we do so, the Bible says, "They shall not be ashamed."

The Bible keeps trying to tell us that the family is for the children. When Noah built the ark, he built for the children.

When Abram left Ur, he left for the children. He became Abraham, the father of the faithful.

When Isaac was spared, he was spared for the children.

When Jacob returned home, he returned for the children.

When Joseph was promoted, he was promoted for the children. He was a blessing when they brought his younger brother.

When Moses was called, he was called for the children.

When Joshua stood firm, he stood for the children. He said, "for me and my house, we will serve the Lord."

When Jeremiah wept, he wept for the children. "Weep ⸍ *the slaying of the daughters of my people."*

When Jesus came, He came for the children. "Suffer the little children to come unto me."

When the Lord wept, He wept for the children.

And one of these days, when our children hit the target, we will sing:

> WHEN ALL GOD'S CHILDREN GET TOGETHER,
> WHAT A DAY OF REJOICING IT WILL BE.
> WE WILL SHOUT HALLELUJAH!
> AND SING THE VICTORY.

A DEAD GIRL AND LAUGHING CROWDS

Text: *Then came one of the rulers of the synagogue, Jairus by name; and seeing him, he fell at his feet, and besought him, saying, "My little daughter is at the point of death. Come and lay your hands on her, so that she may be made well, and live." And he went with him. And a great crowd followed him and thronged about him. And there was a woman who had a flow of blood for twelve years, and who had suffered much under many physicians, and had spent all that she had, and was no better but rather grew worse. She had heard the reports about Jesus, and came up behind him in the crowd and touched his garment. For she said, "If I touch even his garments, I shall be made well." And immediately the hemorrhage ceased; and she was healed of her disease. And Jesus, perceiving in himself that power had gone forth from him, immediately turned about in the crowd, and said, "Who touched my garments?" And his disciples said to him, "You see the crowd pressing around you, and yet you say, 'Who touched me?'" And he looked around to see who had done it. But the woman knowing what had been done, came in fear and trembling and fell down before him, and told him the whole truth. And he said to her, "Daughter, your faith has made you well; go in peace, and be healed of your disease." While he was still speaking, there came from the ruler's house some who said, "Your daughter is dead. Why trouble the Teacher any further?" But ignoring what they said, Jesus said to the ruler of the synagogue, "Do not fear, only believe." And he allowed no one to follow him except Peter and James and John the brother of James. When they came to the house of the ruler of the synagogue, he saw a tumult, and people weeping and wailing loudly. And when he had entered he said to them, "Why do you make a tumult and weep? The girl is not dead but sleeping." And they laughed at him. But he took the child's father and mother and those who were with him, and went in where the child was. Taking her by the hand he said to her, "Talitha cumi"; which means, "Little girl, I say to you, arise." And immediately the girl got up and walked (she was twelve years of age), and they were immediately overcome with amaze-*

*ment. And he strictly charged them that no one should know this, and told them to give her something to eat. (**Mark 5:22-43,** RSV)*

We could probably label our text. " A Litany of Christian Interruptions." For within twenty-plus verses we are met with a multitude of interruptions. Jesus is pictured as pausing on the other side of the sea, with intentions to preach and teach. However, before a word fell from His lips one of the rulers of the synagogue, Jairus by name, interrupted. He came with fatherly concern for an ailing daughter. Jesus responded to Jairus' plea and set out to fulfill the request. But on his way to Jairus' house, Jesus was again interrupted. A woman with an issue of blood and undaunted faith drained healing power from the Master, by touching the hem of His garment. Jesus stopped. He assured the woman that her faith had made her whole.

As Jesus resumed the trip to Jairus' house, again He was interrupted. The negative news from a concerned crowd interrupted Jesus' entourage. They informed Jairus, " Bother Jesus no more! Your daughter is dead."

The negative news failed to discourage Jesus. Thus, He shed Himself of the crowd and took with Him Peter, James, and John. They proceeded to Jairus' house. No sooner than they arrived, Jesus was again interrupted by tumultuous weeping and wailing. A crowd of professional mourners, persons who lived to see others die, interrupted the Savior's travel. They not only interrupted Him with tears, they laughed at Him when He suggested that the dead girl was merely asleep. Yes, many are the interruptions of Jesus in Mark 5:21-43.

We should note, nonetheless, a critical lesson from the Savior: Let nothing interfere with our God-given tasks. We should never be so busy and close-minded that we cannot stop and help somebody, even when on the way to helping somebody else. The church of Jesus Christ should not be so schedule-bound that we cannot positively deal with life's interruptions. For as we travel along life's way, we are certain to have our fair share of interruptions.

Today, however, I would that we focus our attention upon Jairus' daughter. The story of Jairus' daughter is interrupted by another story. Interestingly, both stories are unusually similar. Like the woman with the issue of blood, Jairus' daughter was perceived to be hopelessly ill. They were both characters of tragedy. They were both female, one a grown woman and the other a growing woman. Jairus' daughter was twelve years of age. She was as old as the woman was sick. Or, the woman had been sick, as long as the girl-child had been in the world.

I believe the femaleness of the situation gives to us an angle by which to tell this story. Brethren, there is such a thing as a female story over-and-against the male dominated story. There is a her-story, as well as a his-story. Women have been thrust upon the stage of life, given scripts, and have acted out roles, which were man-made and male satisfying. The results of such man-made scripts and male-satisfying roles is that many women find themselves in hopeless situations. Many of society's women, particularly Black women, are either hemorrhaging through life; i.e., having life drained [or worked] out of them by an insensitive society. Or, like Jairus' daughter they are dead before they ever experience life. Too many of our daughters are already dying from the oppressiveness of our society.

Since we are scheduled to baptize a daughter, a growing woman, let us spend the balance of the message on Jairus' daughter. I believe Jesus helps us with a vision of meaningful life for our daughters. Every sensible father or mother finds little enjoyment out of sick or dead daughters.

Physically and emotionally, no segment of our society is more vulnerable to the wickedness of humanity than girls. Our girls are prime prey for perverts of all kinds. I know that the perverts are also aimed at the boys. We receive daily doses of the horrors of perversions inflicted upon boys. But, historically, girls are watched by the weak and wicked. More girls are abused, raped, misused, and prostituted. Why? Because little girls are usually perceived as the precious and pure element of our society.

Even the Bible makes a lot of noise about the preciousness and purity of girls. The Bible speaks of little girls as virgins, pure and precious. Evil always seeks out the pureness of human society for the ravages of wickedness. The outrage of society can easily be ignited when the abuse of little girls is discovered. Let no man, and, yes, no woman dare lay wicked hands on little girls.

Nonetheless, when we hear of Jairus' daughter, she is sick unto death. Some malicious malady has made her sick. She is hopelessly in the hands of some hellish affliction. Interestingly, the illness is not named. No disease is labeled. An absence of a known disease suggests something more than physical ailment.

As I look through the lenses of history, and gaze upon the female's role in life, I am moved to ponder some suggestions. The femaleness of the situation is no accident. The writer of the gospel is up to something. Let's ask Jairus!

If the little girl did not die a physical death, or by some known disease, how did she die? "Jairus! Why don't you give us an answer. She is your daughter. You know what is wrong with her. You know what killed her. That's why you are out here bothering Jesus. Jairus! Why is your daughter dead? She's dead even before she has experienced life. Why? Jairus, is it possible that since you are a ruler of the synagogue, a big shot in the church, and a man of society, that your daughter died from the disease of imposed expectations. Did you, Jairus, try to shape your daughter into something she was not. When your daughter made mistakes, as all children do, did you beat her with the words: 'a preacher's daughter does not act like that?' Did you, Mr. Jairus, strangle your daughter with goals that not even you could reach?"

I raise Jairus for questioning because we have a lot of dead girls that have been killed by phony parental expectations. Parents are killing children with a false value system. Brothers and Sisters, we kill our children when we raise hell and expect them to be angels. We kill our children when we lie and expect them to tell the truth. We kill our children, when we send them to church and we don't come ourselves. We kill our children, when we expect them to get all "A's" and we will not even pick up a book and read ourselves. We kill our children, by expecting them to be better than we are and we do nothing to better ourselves. The disease of phony parental expectations has left us with a lot of dead girls.

I see in the eyes of young Black girls the haunting look of hopelessness and despair. They are dead before they have experienced life. D.O.A., dead on arrival, if you please. Like Jeremiah, "Behold, the voice of the cry of the daughters of my people...."

Well, Jairus, maybe you did not kill your daughter with parental expectations. Maybe you were a good ol' Dad, with modest expectations. But if you did not kill her, who did? Your daughter is dead.

"What about you, oh relentless society? Society! You have been known to kill daughters. You have been known to destroy the potential of children with your insensitive politics, your chauvinistic government, your unequal economics, and your sexist education. Your structures of home, state, and church have been demonized to the destruction of women." Maybe the daughter is dead from the crushing trap of tradition, and the fixed limitations of an unjust society. In a society that defines people by sex, race, creed, and color, it is so easy to kill and destroy our daughters. Yes, in a society that tells you what to do, where to go and where not to go; what you can be and what you cannot be, as well as what to wear—it can kill you!

Under the banner of "my country tis of thee, sweet land of liberty," is an America that destroys daughters. To you, my Brethren, we need to quit feeling threatened by strong Black women. If we, as a people, have made any progress it is because of strong Black women. Our freedom will never be complete until the freedom of women is complete. Martin Luther King, Jr., once said, "Injustice anywhere is a threat to justice everywhere" and sexism is as unjust as racism.

Too many of our daughters are dead before they can experience life because society has already defined their lives. The trap of tradition without truth tramples the life out of our daughters. The devil has been known to crush us by stomping out potentials and possibilities.

Young daughters of Africa, rise high as the sky and let no one deaden your lofty ambitions. Don't die a sex object, a breeding mare, or a dressed up mannequin. Be somebody! Live out your ambitions, in the spirit of Christ, for He has come to raise up even the dead. You are not limited to nursing—be a doctor! You are not limited to public school teaching—be a college professor! You are not limited to cleaning houses, buy and sell houses—be a real estate agent! You are not limited to typewriters and switchboards, climb the corporate ladders and own businesses. Little Sisters, you are not limited to the choirs, ushers, and mothers' board. If God calls you, step forth and preach Christ. "There is neither Jew nor Greek, there is neither bond nor free, there is neither male nor female; for we are all one in Christ."

I would even add strong daughters will also mean strong

sons. Our daughters, as liberated and whole persons, will become liberated and whole mothers, who will produce liberated and whole children. A good mother will always produce good children.

"Jairus, your daughter is dead!" As I bring to closure this message, look with me at the laughing crowd. Jesus comes upon the scene and is met with tumultuous weeping and wailing. He entered into the house and said unto them, "Why do you make a tumult and weep? The child is not dead but sleeping." Almost in the prose of Shakespeare, Jesus suggested that the crowd was " making much ado about nothing."

It is interesting that as soon as Jesus spoke these words, they laughed Him to scorn. It is interesting how folk can cry one minute and laugh in the next. People can be down one minute, but put somebody down in the next. Deep inside we are not even fooled by the tragedies of tradition, particularly, how it makes us laugh when we ought to cry and cry when we ought to laugh. Programmed tears can so quickly become words of scorn. The Greek meaning of the word "scorn" suggests that they put Jesus down. In other words, they ridiculed Him. They despised His words. They rejected His insight. They put Jesus down.

The laughing crowd put Jesus down, because they would rather have a dead girl than a resurrecting Jesus. Like so many of us, they would rather engage in the traditions of death than to receive a word from the Prince of Life. They believed that death has the last word, rather than God having the last word.

Notice, how Jesus deals with the laughing crowd. He simply put them out. If a miracle was to take place, Jesus knew that the dead girl and the laughing crowd could not occupy the same room. If work was to take place, playing folk can't run with serious folk. The church needs to know that there is a difference between a playground and the workplace, the carnival and the vineyard, and between clowns and laborers. Playing Christians get in the way of serious Christians. The church has far too many playing folk. If we are to ever do great things for the Lord, playing folk will have to get out of the room. If we are to ever grow in grace, playing folk must get out of the room. If we are to ever have witnessing power, playing folk must get out of the room. If dead folk are to be raised, the playing folk must get out of the room. There's no room for playing, when Jesus comes into the rooms of our defeats and disappointments.

The Bible says Jesus put them out. He then took the father and the mother, both parents, and the serious disciples into the room where the daughter lay. Upon arriving in the room, He reached down and took the child by the hand, and said, "Talitha cumi, ...Daughter, rise." And immediately the daughter got up and began to walk." As she walked in the newness of life, Jesus commanded that they give her something to eat.

On any given Sunday morning, some young daughter lets Jesus into the room of her life. She professes hope in Christ and submits to baptism. We take her down into a watery grave and she comes up into the newness of life. Yes, they rise up and walk a new walk. They talk a new talk. They sing a new song. Yet, if young daughters are to really live, we will need to feed them. Dead folk don't eat, but living folk need to eat.

So I need to tell you, as did Jesus, give our daughters something to eat. Not bread alone, but every word that proceeds from the mouth of God.

> *If we feed her truth, she will live truthfully.*
> *If we feed her facts, she will live in reality.*
> *If we feed her love, she will be more loving.*

If we feed her forgiveness, she will be forgiving.
If we feed her tolerance, she will live with patience.
If we feed her praise, she will live with confidence.
If we feed her fairness, she will live believing in justice.
If we feed her security, she will live by faith and not by
    sight.
If we feed her God's word, she will walk in God's way.
If we feed her prayer, she will grow tall on bended knees.
If we feed her Jesus, when we have done all that we
    can do, we can say:
"Bread from heaven, Bread from heaven,
 Feed [her] until she wants no more."

WHERE ARE WE GOING WITH OUR CHILDREN?

Text: *And they were bringing children to him, that he might touch them; and the disciples rebuked them. But when Jesus saw it he was indignant, and said to them, "Let the children come to me, do not hinder them; for to such belongs to the kingdom of God. Truly, I say to you, whoever does not receive the kingdom of God like a child shall not enter it." And he took them in his arms and blessed them, laying his hands upon them. (Mark 10:13-16,* RSV)

Where are we going with our children? We struggle to feed them and dress them. We worry over their progress, or lack of progress. We even agonize over whether or not we are doing a good job of parenting. We have raised our voices, stomped our feet, pulled out our hair, and spanked their bottoms. But where are we going with our children? We have recently assumed the helpless posture that today's children are strange, unusual, unique, and impossible. We are puzzled by their responses to our style of parenting, our gestures of love, and even our assertions of parental authority. Parents, all over, are not too convinced that we are doing the right things for the children. We breathe sighs of relief whenever one child halfway does what he or she is supposed to do. But where are we going with our children?

This question is raised for two reasons. First of all, where we go with them is far more impacting than where we send them. We have been doing a lot of sending and not going with them. We send them to school. We send them to "whoever's" house. We send them to play. We send them to the store. We even send them to church. Where we go with them says more about our real intention for them than anywhere we may send them. Furthermore, if we are not going with them , where we are sending them may not be the best place for them to be. Secondly, the story of our text strongly suggests that parent-people have historically thought it wise to get children to Jesus. However, the effort to get children to Jesus has always been frustrating.

Chapter 10 of Mark's witness includes within it some of the most powerful statements concerning the spiritual attitudes of those who best represent the Jesus community. The matters of marital relationships plagued both Pharisees and disciples. The relationship of disciples to possessions was dramatically lifted up in the rich young ruler. The servant model was pointed out as the only true attitude for a disciple of Jesus Christ. Gratitude and the willingness to redemptively suffer was also powerfully imaged and dramatized. Then here come some folk with a group of noisy, restless, busy, inquisitive children. Jesus used the children as the ultimate models of kingdom candidates.

Rufus Jones made note in his last book, A Call To What Is Vital, that the prophet's task was to bring religion up-to-date. He noted that religion has the awful tendency to become stale, senile, and out of step with current realities. Religion has a bad habit of looking over its shoulder, becoming obsessed with ancient rituals and practices. The prophetic urgency is always a call to God's people to bring their religion up-to-date.

Jesus was certainly more than a prophet. Yet, He engaged in the activities and performances of a prophet. He was viewed as prophet by enemies and friends. When He inquired as to who people were calling Him, the answer was "as one of the prophets." People saw in Jesus the prophetic urgings of pulling religion up-to-date. The cleansing of the temple was bringing religion up-to-date. The new wine in new bottles metaphorically implied up-dating religion. His challenging responses to "You say" or "Your fathers say"; but "I say" was up-dating religion. When a woman was caught in adultery, law-filled religion said, "Stone her." However, the up-dated religion of grace replied, "He, who is without sin, cast the first stone." An outdated faith placed worship days and rituals over human needs; but an up-dated religion understands that "the Sabbath was made for man, and man was not made for the Sabbath." An out-dated religion locks in upon the past expressions of Abraham, but a religion updated cries, "Before Abraham was, I am." Even the loyalty of family was updated in Jesus. He said, "My mother and father, sisters and brothers [are not limited to blood-ties] but expanded to those who do the will of my Father."

It is quite strange that the updating pull of Jesus had not captured the vision of His disciples. How did the disciples miss the fact that Jesus was intensely interested in children? I have begun to grow uneasy with the church whenever the question is raised about where are men? Or teenagers? Or responsible and gifted young adults? These questions are troublesome because they always point the church's eyes outside of the church. We are essentially asking where are those outside of our ranks who should be inside? The problem with that kind of question is that it fools the church into trying to reach out, without first looking deep within.

A careful and probing look within may allow us to see that an invigorating faith requires intergenerational inclusiveness, where children are viewed as vital participants. Whenever children are considered as vital components of the church's pilgrimage, the church goes places. Children provide the church with an on-the-scene glimpse of the future. They provide us a freshness, a youthfulness, an energetic boost, a foretaste of faith adventures. We shall be because the children are.

But like the disciples we have set boundaries around

children's involvement in the church. And whenever the participation of children is categorized and regulated, the vitality of our faith is minimized. The energetic possibilities of the faith community are severely limited when we limit the children.

Maybe the disciples were so into who they were that the presence of the children was viewed as a hindrance. "Let's hold them out here for a while. Let them sing to entertain us. Let's not concern ourselves with them right now, because it is all about us!" Children in such an arrangement are viewed as mere objects and not as persons of worth and dignity. They are but religious stimulants for folk who are literally bored with themselves. Whenever the participation level of children is minimized we take away from our own potential.

Children love outdoors. They have a natural relationship with the earth. So when we fail to adequately include them our own energies are wasted by in-house squabbling, rather than being enhanced by the life-forces that are external to our gathering. Children instinctively know that there is more going on out there than there will ever be in here.

The words of our text clearly suggest that the inclusion of children in the Jesus community demands that we take Jesus seriously. We take Jesus so seriously that we endure pain so that the children can get to Jesus. I don't want to spend much time on this, but it did occur to me that persons who already have made contact with Jesus should not have any problem with other folk getting to Jesus. Children should not be a threat to adults who are supposed to already have a relationship with Jesus. Some adults are threatened by others who may get something that they do not have.

One of the pains that the church least wants to confront

is the possibility that it has been wrong! Jesus clearly lifts before the disciples that fact that they are wrong in their understanding about children's relationship to Him. If children are not being powerfully impacted by Jesus, it may well be that we are wrong. We are wrong in our models of ministering to children. We are wrong if we think the only ministry to children is to place them in some choir. I know we don't want to hear it, but we may be wrong in our understanding of youth in relation to Christ and the church. We certainly cannot afford to rush into some of these good-intentioned, uninformed, non-examined assumptions. So many believe that a party, a trip, a picnic, an orgy of good times will hold today's youth. Too often these assumptions have proved wrong and disastrous. Yet, these old models of read the Bible, stay in church, and be good are inadequate, out-of-date, and grossly incorrect.

However, Jesus challenges us to do the painful—suffer some for the children. Change our ways of thinking, of doing business, and what we believe is right for children. We need to see that what we think is not as important as what motivates and informs our thinking. Our selfishness, pettiness, narrowness, and faithlessness mold and shape our thinking. As a result, the children are kept a distance from the fullness of life. Our children need more than food, a place to sit, play, and sleep. They need more than cute clothes, robes, and Sunday manners. They need a vision of life, a force in their hearts that will hold their heads up and inspire them to creatively dream. They need persons who dare to carry them into adventures of faith, where none has travelled. They need a stability of community that does not fall during the storms of life. Children need some faith models who know the life-changing, situation-rearranging power of almighty God.

Also adult-disciples, who take Jesus seriously, will remove themselves from obstructing the path to Jesus. We, adults, have historically made it difficult for children to get in touch with Jesus. We are so hypocritical, so phony, and so insincere. Where are we going with our children, when we ignore what is noble and right and sensible? I just left a National Council of Churches meeting where I was called upon to help phrase a resolution. The resolution was a call for all denominations in America and Canada to declare smoke-free zones all facilities where denominations gather. Seriously, Brothers and Sisters, how in the world can we get children to Jesus when we assault our bodies with poisonous gases, in spite of NO SMOKING signs? Every smoking adult ought to be ashamed whenever a child sees you smoke. We ought not parade our weaknesses before children. An adult who smokes in front of children is a self-destructive, genocidal maniac, who does not care about life, nor the life of children. If we are going to smoke around the church, why not build a bar and let's drink around the church? What's the difference? They are both poisons that have been legalized by a profit-motivated society.

Jesus exhorted His mistaken disciples to get out of the children's way. I am greatly pained by adults with low self-esteem, who abuse the life-forces of children. I was busing from Louisiana when I heard a young woman mercilessly curse a child. The names she called that child I have reserved for no one. Yet, her esteem was so low that she built herself up by beating down her child. Where are we going with our children, when we don't even know where we are going ourselves?

The inclusion of children in the Jesus community demands that adults take Jesus so seriously that they understand the child-connection to the kingdom. Brothers and Sisters, the church points to a reality beyond itself. The church offers clues to the dynamics of the Kingdom. Jesus connected the child to citizenship in the Kingdom. He said, "Such is the kingdom. Verily, I say unto you, whosoever shall not receive the kingdom of God as a child, he shall not enter therein."

A child is the most faithful among us. A child expresses love most honestly. A child can be the most trusting of all human beings. Children are the most dependent of creatures. A child exudes reckless joy and endless hope. A child will do all, give all, hope all, and try all, out of his/her love for the parent. A child possesses the spiritual innocence necessary for the kingdom.

Children are not normally deceitful, greedy, and cunning. We never hear of children playing petty politics, always seeking selfish advantage. Jesus was so serious about the child-kingdom connection, He told one man, "You must be born again." I heard one writer speaking to a kingdom-bound church. He said, "My little children, these things I write unto you..., we have an advocate with the Father, Jesus Christ the righteous." The Psalmist said, "Out of the mouth of babes comes perfect praise." Children represent God's password to the kingdom. Where are we going with our children? If our children go to hell, we have much to do with carrying them there.

The disciples took Jesus seriously. They assisted in getting the children to Jesus. They made certain that the children established a relationship with Jesus. The Bible says, "And he took them in his arms and blessed them, laying hands upon them." The words used here are the same as those used to set apart persons for special service. The term "laying his hands on them" is the same phrase used in the so-called "ordination" of deacons in Acts 6:6. The point seems to be that Jesus' touch had a continuing impact upon the children's lives, particularly as manifested in the life of the church. His touch identified them as significant persons in the business of redemption. Jesus gave them a place of special significance in kingdom enterprises.

I have three children, with whom God has blessed our household. All of my children are unique and have unique needs. I do not try to treat them all equally; I try to serve them all adequately. My eldest daughter is brilliant and steady. She has unusual mental prowess and a hunger to learn. However, she is too quick to get bored and too easily influenced. My son is independent and very strong-willed. He, too, could probably learn anything if he applied himself. However, he is too easily distracted. He is a sucker for not paying attention. My youngest daughter is very special. She has learned to survive in a world, without our initially being aware of her special-ness. She has been with us for nearly four years and we just discovered that she has some hearing loss. All of her life she has been reading lips and interpreting gestures and hearing inaudible sounds. She was on her way to establishing herself a world, where she would let in whoever she chose.

Now I could send my children to specialists. We could send them to schools and academics. Karen and I have made church primary in their young lives. We don't send them; we go with them. Yet, we are both aware that specialists cannot save them and that schools are no guarantee of goodness. We also understand that the church can pervert them and distort reality. So we have committed ourselves to make Jesus real in their lives. We have made up our minds to take them to Jesus. We have made up our minds to suffer some and deny ourselves, so that the children can meet Jesus. If I act a little pushy, at times, please forgive me. I have some children in tow, who need to see Jesus.

I know if Jesus touches them, His touch will hold them.

If Jesus touches them, His touch will keep them. If Jesus places them in His arm, nothing will separate them from His love. If Jesus guides their paths, they will never go astray. Notice, I refer to Jesus and not the church. However, if Jesus blesses them, they will be a blessing to the church. Furthermore, if Jesus blesses them, I, too, will be blessed. I don't want to hinder them from His touch.

When He touches, He sets apart.
When He touches, He lifts up.
When He touches, He sanctifies.
When He touches, He strengthens.
When He touches, He glorifies.

Once the Lord blesses the children, the children bless us. Hallelujah! Praise God!

WHERE ARE WE GOING WITH OUR BOYS?

Text: *But Sarah saw the son of Hagar the Egyptian, whom she had borne to Abraham, playing with her son Isaac. So she said to Abraham, "Cast out this slave woman with her son; for the son of this slave woman shall not be heir with my son Isaac." And the thing was very displeasing to Abraham on account of his son. But God said to Abraham, "Be not displeased because of the lad and because of your slave woman; whatever Sarah says to you, do as she tells you, for through Isaac shall your descendants be named. And I will make a nation of the son of the slave woman also, because he is your offspring." So Abraham rose early in the morning, and took bread and skin of water, and gave it to Hagar, putting it on her shoulder, along with the child, and sent her away. And she departed, and wandered in the wilderness of Beer-sheba. When the water in the skin was gone, she cast the child under one of the bushes. Then she went, and sat down over against him a good way off, about the distance of a bowshot; for she said, "Let me not look upon the death of the child." And as she sat over against him, the child lifted up his voice and wept. And God heard the voice of the lad, and the angel of God called to Hagar from heaven, and said to her, "What troubles you, Hagar? fear not; for God has heard the voice of the lad where he is. Arise, lift up the lad, and hold him fast with your hand; for I will make him a great nation." Then God opened her eyes, and she saw a well of water; and she went, and filled the skin with water, and gave the lad to drink. And God was with the lad, and he grew up; and became an expert with the bow. He lived in the wilderness of Paran; and his mother took a wife for him from the land of Egypt. (**Genesis 21:9-21** RSV)*

I sometimes wonder why God called me to be a preacher within the ambiguous uncertainties of the Black Baptist church. If I understand anything about preaching, I understand that preaching leads to life-changing actions.

The lives of people are confronted with creative possibilities when the gospel is preached. For the Black community, preaching provides liberating perspectives upon the lives of persons who live out their lives within oppressive arrangements. Preaching opens up the grace-filled potentials of life being powerfully experienced in relation to God, and God's will in the affairs of humanity. Folk, who experience preaching, are people of action. However, the actions of the Black church have been woefully slow.

I make no claim to great preaching. I do, however, work hard and try my best. As a senior sage once advised Caesar Clark, "I study as if there is no such thing as the Holy Spirit and I stand as if there is nothing but the Holy Spirit." My dilemma remains: why are we so slow to act when confronted by so much preaching? Has the Black church grown immune to preaching? Or, are we content to remain inactive in spite of the action-packed mandates of preaching? Jeremiah painfully stated, "The harvest is past, the summer is ended; but we are not saved." My pain is: "The preacher has come, the preaching has ended; but we have not moved."

My pain is intensified when I view the crumbling landscape of the Black community. The landscape has crumbled when children are daily subjected to the most demeaning existence. The landscape has crumbled when the craziness of this world is dumped upon the laps of the innocent young. We have become poor caretakers of our future. We are mishandling our tomorrows. We are making certain that we cause the miscarriage our possibilities, by neglecting the development of children. My question to God and you: Why preach when we are so reluctant to move and commit ourselves to the obvious? Has our preaching become mere entertainment for a people who have literally thrown in the towel on liberation, and only want to be drugged on some soothing words?

I probably would not preach in the church, if it was all up to me. I would join some revolutionary movement and empty myself with those who live on the cutting edge. But the Bible has a way of sobering the intoxications of idealism. The Bible brings me back down into the earthiness of my journey. I find in the Bible why I had better preach, even when it does not look like any redemptive actions are forthcoming. The Bible gives me marching orders to shout, even when the troops are not obeying. God issues forth grace-filled commands primarily for those who are prone to inaction. In light of the divine imperative of the Bible, I want to lift from scripture an obvious pain with a gospel solution. There is a painful reality, which we are called to act upon. If we do not act, we bring pain upon the heart of God. If we do not act, we make mockery of the Cross. If we do not act, we make powerless the church. If we do not act, we risk excluding ourselves from being whole persons and a strong, respected nation.

The story of Ishmael leads me to ask you where are we going with our boys? My use of the term "boy" is in no way dehumanizing. I am not saying "boy" with the derision of our oppressors. I am using the term "boy" to refer to those young Black men in our midst, who are infants, adolescents, pre-teens, and early teens. I speak of those young Black males who are, for the most part, dependent upon adults for their basic welfare. I speak of those young Black males whom we discipline, rebuke, and admonish. I speak of those young Blacks who, of necessity, have to be under the supervision of some adult person. Where are we going with these young, energetic, intelligent, creative men-in-the-making? Where are we going with our boys?

The church should be clear about where it is going with cargo, so precious to our welfare. Our concern should be intensified when the general feelings are that boys are the candidates for the worst in our society. Even as I speak, we have more young Black males in prison than we have in college. The next generation of inmates, our boys, are known by name and address. Less than half of our boys in high school will finish with a High School diploma. According to the U. S. census, young Black males are more likely to be murdered than young whites. Black males represent over 50% of the prison population, whereas the entire Black population in the country is but 13%. Black men lead the list in six leading causes of death: homicide, heart attacks, cancer, suicide, strokes, and accidents. Most of our youth, by the time they are seventeen, will have very little interest in the archaic ways of the Black church. Where are we going with our boys?

When I read the Ishmaelic epic, certain truths powerfully speak to us as a people. Ishmael was the son of an oppressed society. In fact, oppressive arrangements brought him into the world. His mother was a victim of oppression and his father was a prisoner of the oppressive culture. When the child of the oppressor was born, Ishmael's existence was endangered. Even under a spell of divine providence, the oppressive society promoted practices detrimental to Ishmael's well being. Sarah insisted, and Abraham assisted, in placing Ishmael in a life-threatening situation. He was the reason for Ishmael and his mother being exiled from the privilege of equality—not his mother. It was Ishmael's relation to his father that was threatening to Isaac, resulting in the banishment of Ishmael and Hagar.

One of the things that God always expects is that the community of the faithful will adequately provide for the dependent in its midst. The children, our boys, are to be provided with adequate experiences and necessities so that they may mature into responsible citizens of faith. As people of an oppressed community, we must come to realize that oppressors will never give our boys an equal opportunity. It is foolish for us to think that white folk are going to educate our boys to take jobs from their sons. I have been Black every day of my life and I have yet to receive a respectable job from whites, after having competed with another white of lesser qualifications. Hagar's child is always banished from equal opportunity.

Some of you have read this story and are probably saying, "Abraham did give the woman bread and water for their journey." Yet, when has bread and water ever been enough? The story allows us to see the inadequacy of Abraham's welfare system. Hagar and Ishmael did not get very far on those meager supplies. Abraham, in fact, did have good intentions. But we need to learn that good intentions alone often produce inadequate results, especially when preparing boys to be men. I believe that the church has had good intentions. We have boys' classes. We even allow young brothers to sing in choirs. On special days we allow them a morsel of the program. The truth is, however, that our good intentions have not slowed down the rising prison population, reduced drug abusers, baby makers, cool dudes, and irresponsible teens, who live off of an OPP philosophy. (You older folk would probably not know the meaning of OPP.) Good intentions without illumination, sacrifice and commitment never have long-standing results. Choirs cannot hold young boys when those who lead choirs lack commitment. Sunday School classes cannot hold young boys, when those who teach are habitually late for class.

Hagar took the meager morsels from Abraham's welfare system and went on her single-parent way. A woman and a male-child are sent out to make it in a wild and wicked world. In fact, the text says, "And she departed, and wandered about in the wilderness...." I will never stop applauding the marvelous jobs many single women are doing, and have done, in raising male children. The half has yet to be told concerning African American single-parenting women. Yet, when trying to raise up a nation, leaving boys in the hands of women can be risky business. The strength of sisters has been admirable; but it takes a strong Black man to raise a Black boy to be a Black man in white America. Underline strong Black man, for in the words of our folk "It takes more than breath and britches to be a man."

My young people recommend that I do not view certain movies. Twelve and thirteen year-olders view certain movies, but they don't want me to view them. I go anyway. The Lord has blessed me to view movies for more than what is being shown. I look for the depth message behind what is being shown. In the recent blockbuster, "Boyz N' the Hood," the message of the movies was disturbingly true. The movie was not just about the Black neighborhood and Black teens. It was about boys trying to be men through guns, drugs, and sex organs. Guns, drugs, and irresponsible sex are the weapons of our oppressor to facilitate Black genocide through crime,abuse, and incurable disease. Such a wilderness environment is much too difficult for women to go at it alone. Positive Black males must find creative ways to raise our boys into Black men.

Hagar went. The food ran out. The water supply was exhausted. She was overwhelmed by despair and placed the boy under a bush to die. She could not bear to see her son die, so she went opposite him and lifted her voice in despair. As I listen to mothers, I often hear voices of despair. Mothers (and fathers) have given up on the life possibilities of young Black males. Too many parents have lost hope in the ability of their sons to make it in America. The bushes of despair are full of our boys, while at the same time the blessings of opportunity are far too slim.

Only a few will make it in the wilderness of the NFL. Only a few will ever make it in the NBA, or professional baseball. Only a few will make it into the entertainment business. Presently, only a few are making it in high government. Where are we going with our boys? The story does not end with a mother in tears, nor with a dead boy under a bush. God doesn't work like that. It appears that when the woman exhausted her resources, God started His resources. Someone has said, "Human extremity is God's opportunity." I am excited about this text, for it directs the church where she ought to be going with our boys. This text represents marching orders for the black church. It is an action-packed agenda for ministering to Black boys.

The text says that "God heard the lad crying." My strong belief is that the church ultimately represents God in the world. If the church is to embody God in the world, the church must begin to hear who God hears. It may be that we are so busy listening to adults cry, listening to one another, that we have failed to hear who God hears. Most of this abhorrent behavior among our boys is neither badness, nor madness. It is the cries of boys who feel left alone under the bushes of parental despair. Drug use is crying. Violent acts are crying. Rebellion is crying. Gang-banging is crying. Stubbornness is crying. We must get beneath the bushes of their behavior and hear the cries. I recently purchased a book, entitled, Where Grown Men Cry. Grown men cry when thrust in prison bushes. The truth is crying grown men are just boys who have been crying for a long time.

The text also helps us to see that crying boys are heard, only when we go where they are. God heard the voice of the boy where he was. We must leave the lofts of our adult assumptions and go where the children are. Maybe Ishmael was really crying out of the confusing elements of the adults in his world. His real pain could have been the pain of adults living in constant conflict. Children internalize the tensions and hostilities of adults, long before they are able to make sense out of it. If we are to go where the boys are, we may painfully discover that they are crying as a result of adult madness. Most of what hurts our boys is inflicted upon them by a hostile adult environment. God expects for us to go where they are, even if it means confronting the mad ugliness of ourselves. God expects for us to be where the boys are, so that we may hear their cries.

I love the Lord, because He heard my cry
And pitied evr'y groan.

When God heard the boy's cry, God's response was to open the eyes of his mother. The church could well point boys in the right direction, by providing eye-opening experiences which allow adults to see the liberating possibilities of God. Hagar's eyes opened and allowed her to see herself differently, the world differently, and even the boy differently. One thing the church should provide for those in despair are visions of hope and life. Persons in despair need to see that they are not slaves to situations and circumstances. People may mistreat us, even abuse us, but we do not have to be slaves to the negatives of life.

Our biggest challenge is to open the eyes of adults, so that they can see themselves differently. The world can be a great friend, just as it can be a grueling foe. The water was there all of the time, but she could not see out of the eyes of low self-esteem and negative self-worth. Young Black males would see themselves more positively, when Black adults start seeing themselves in a more positive light. Liberating possibilities are all around us, but we cannot see them through the lenses of low self-esteem. For those with eyes to see, freedom is in the air. Everything we need to build boys into men is present in our world, the world of the Black church. The church can embody the presence of God, even in the midst of a social wilderness. Notice, Ishmael and Hagar never left the wilderness. In fact, Ishmael mastered the wilderness. Where we are can become a promised land, when eyes are opened to God's possibilities.

Where are we going with our boys? I know where we should go. And if you have paid any attention you, too, should know. Our boys can become men even in an oppressive society. The text says that Ishmael lived, became a man, became a husband, became a father, became responsible, became creative—he mastered skills. The reason he became a man was because God spoke marching orders to the adult in his life. God told her, **Arise, lift up the lad, and hold him by the hand; for I will make a great nation of him."** Brothers and Sisters, the Lord wants us to get up. " Arise!" Get up from our slothfulness. Get up from our insensitivity. Get up from our excuses. Get up from our sense of inadequacy. Get up from narrow-mindedness. Get up from slave-thinking. Get up and go where the boys are.

If we get up, we can lift the boys up. "Arise, lift up the lad." When we rise above pettiness, we can lift up boys into greatness. When we rise above selfishness, we can lift boys into creative service. When we rise above greed, we can lift boys into generosity. When we rise above ignorance, we can lift boys into truth and knowledge. When we rise above dependency, we can lift boys into independency. When we rise above gloom and despair, we can lift boys toward hope and glory.

And when we lift them up, hold on to them! Take them by the hand. Our boys need strong hands. Our boys need caring hands. Our boys need giving hands. Our boys need praying hands.

"Precious Lord, take my hand; lead me on, help me to stand."

The story says that Hagar acted on the Lord's word.

She did what God told her to do. The result was: God was with the lad. God was with the boy. Brothers and Sisters, the Lord will more likely be with our children, if we do as God directs us. I want God to be with the boys. There was another boy. His name was Emmanuel, which means "God with us." Jesus was a boy of the ghetto. He was a boy of oppression. He was a boy of a teenage mother. He was a boy in a confused world of confused adults. But, He grew up to be a man. He grew up to be my Savior. He grew up to be my Lord. He grew up to carry a rugged Cross. He grew up to lighten heavy burdens. He grew up through hate to love. He grew up through scorn to care. He grew up, even though buried in a tomb. He overcame death and the grave. He took the sting out of death. God is with us!

God is with the boys!
God is with us! Hallelujah! Praise God!

CAN MOTHER GET A WITNESS?

Text: *"Her children rise up and call her blessed; Her husband also and he praises her.... Train up a child in the way he should go, and when he is old he will not depart from it."* (**Proverbs 31:28; 22:6,** New King James Version)

The most loved person in the world is mother. The affections of the most rugged individuals come into clear focus once extended toward mother. I know of no person that claims and receives more credit for individuals' successes than mother. When we consider the words of the poet:

> THEY SAY THAT A MAN IS MIGHTY,
>   HE GOVERNS LAND AND SEA
> HE WIELDS A MIGHTY SCEPTER
>   O'ER LESSER POWERS THAN HE.
> BUT A MIGHTY POWER AND STRONGER
>   MAN FROM HIS THRONE HAS HURLED:
> FOR THE HAND THAT ROCKS THE CRADLE
>   IS THE HAND THAT RULES THE WORLD.

Clearly the poet sees that the route to a person's soul passes through mother.

I am beginning to have a lot of reservations about designated days to express love to certain people. Showing people that we appreciate them should not be regulated by calendars. It is most unfortunate that sin has rendered us so self-centered that we must schedule days in which to express love and appreciation. A mother should be the one person who knows that she is always appreciated.

The words of the Proverbs are most instructive in moving us beyond such superficial expressions of appreciation for mother. The words of this wise sage inform us that what means more to mother is to have some witnesses, some folk who can give living witness of their appreciation for mother. Proverbs says that her children rise up and call her blessed. One translation says that "her children arise and call her blessed." The emphasis is on the children, who have been blessed. Motherhood presupposes children. Children make mothers, as much as mothers make children.

The true witness of mothers are children who are blessed. Blessed children are those who adequately reach their God-given potential. Mothers are not really interested in appreciation days. Mothers are more interested in children who become what they can potentially become. A witness for mother is a child with a fulfilled life. Can mother get a witness?

We must move to say that the failure of children to reach their God-given potential damages the witness of mother. The shame of most mothers is shameful children. Can mother get a witness? The children who deny what mother affirms do not give mother a witness. Mother believes you can, but you live like you cannot. Mother can't get a witness. Mother believes you know better, but you act like you don't know any better. Mother can't get a witness. Mother gives us her all, we waste all she gives. Mother can't get a witness. Mother shows you what is good, but you do what is evil. Mother can't get a witness. Mother points you to high ground, but you choose the low ground. Mother can't get a witness. Mother wants you to be a man, but you prefer to be a boy. Mother wants you to be lady, but you choose to be less than a lady. In all of this, mother can't get a witness.

In the case of the Black mother, her best efforts can lead to naught. White America was never designed to produce positive, productive Black children. There is nothing here to help Black children to become strong Black men and women. A young female preacher poetically stated:

"Raising a Black child ain't no easy thing, you have to call on Jesus and listen to the angels sing."

Black mothers have had to raise children in the most

116

difficult of circumstances, often all by themselves. They have led anti-drug crusades. They have combated crime, made poverty liveable, and have sacrificed personal ambitions for the children. They have been the primary supporters of a male-deficient church. Many of the failures of Black children are the result of a job that has been near impossible. Black mothers raising healthy, positive, productive children in a racist, crime-ridden, crack-filled, despair-darkened society is virtually impossible. It's hard for Mother to get a witness.

I was raised in a time when to insult mother was a sure fight. No one ever talked about another person's mother, unless he/she wanted to fight. Today, Blacks bash mothers even on television screens for white-folk entertainment and commercial stimulation. Mother cannot get a witness like that. Mother cannot get a witness when she runs with the children, dates who the daughters date, smokes what the son smokes, and drinks what the men drink. Too many young Black mothers emotionally destroy Black children, by condemning the children for their failures. Mother can't get a witness. I know numerous blacks who have refused to better themselves as a protest against an abusive mother. It is not always mother's fault, but sometimes mother cannot get a witness because of her faults. When mother never allows children to grow up and be independent and responsible—mother can't get a witness.

Again, the Proverbs instruct us as to what constitutes a blessed mother. We are told about a mother who really feels appreciated. An appreciated mother is one who gets a witness from blessed children. Children, who arise, can be a witness for mother. An adequate witness for mother is to duplicate in our lives what mother invested in us. The first thing that mother invested in us was unselfish love. The very first thing that we understand about mother is that she loves us. Mother can get a witness when love comes out in her children.

The love I refer to is not romantic. It is so much like the love of God that mother is usually our first image of God. Mother gives sacrificial love from our early crying to our bed dying. Mother got up out of her sleep, fed us, and cared for us. There was nothing we did so dirty that Mother would not put her hands in it, in an effort to clean us up. Mother would love us, when all had forsaken us. She understood when all others misunderstood.

Mother can get a witness if love can become more real in our lives. If we can be more giving, mother can get a witness. If we can be more understanding, mother can get a witness. If we could take our eyes off of ourselves, then mother can get a witness. If we can get some redemptive dirt on us, as we clean one another up, then mother can get a witness. If we could protect one another more, mother can get a witness. If we could be warm, mother can get a witness. The love we live gives a witness to our appreciation of mother.

Children call mother blessed when they, secondly, give witness to mother's vision. Mothers are great visionaries. My own mother was most supportive when I started moving forward, because my forward moving was her deep desire. Mothers desire that their children move forward. Pity the child who has a backward mother. Mothers are future-oriented. They want better for their children. Mother can get a witness when we start being more visionary.

The potential of children is never realized in the present. To raise children is to essentially invest in the future. The activities of our todays are installments for the future. Mother's vision for us was that we would make the world a better place than it has been for them. It is not a vision cluttered with material possessions. It is a vision that sees Black children being free to become what all children are free to become.

I was so moved in a recent rereading of <u>Uncle Tom's Cabin</u>. It has a moving account of a mother's vision for her child. Liza, the slave woman, could not live knowing that her son was being sold away from her. Liza, fueled by her vision of freedom for her child, bundled him up and fled into the night. When pursued by slave hunters, Liza leaped into the Ohio River and used broken chunks of ice as a bridge for freedom. The sharp chunks of ice cut the shoes off of her feet, but the vision she held for the child carried her across the river.

Mother can get a witness, if we can pursue visions of freedom for our children. If we can see our children living in a world that is fit to live in, then mother can get a witness. Mother can get a witness if we brave the slippery paths in pursuit of lofty goals. If we would courageously flee from the bondages of dark falsehood to the light of God's truth, Mother can get a witness. If we would empty ourselves into the futures of our children, mother can get a witness. Can mother get a witness?

Children call mother blessed, thirdly, when they give witness to Mother's faith. The very fact that a mother exists is an expression of faith. Mothering is faith in flesh. No mother knows what she is getting into when she births a child. Children are no guaranteed thing. You can give your very best to a child and he/she may still break your heart. Mothering can be truly described as "the substance of things hoped for, and the evidence of things not seen." No wonder mothers fill the Lord's house, trusting in God. More prayers are uttered by mothers than any one. Mothers believe that the God of the heavens can help her with the children of her heart. Mothers have been convinced of the wondrous powers of the Lord.

So many young people think that mother would be pleased if he/she became rich and famous. Some of us have believed that mother desired that we be better than others. A lot of Blacks try to show appreciation to mother with cash, cars, homes, jewelry, and things. A lot of folk have married certain people because they thought that was what Mamma wanted. The truth is mother will be satisfied if you and I would just serve Mother's God. Proverbs 22:6 speaks of a training that focuses on God. Mother's God has brought us. Mother's God has kept us. Mother's God did for us what no other power could do. If not for Mother's God, not even Mother would have made it.

The potential of children is determined by their relationship with God. Children will rise no further than the wings of their witness. Brothers and Sisters, mother can get a witness, if we trust in God. Mother can get a witness, if we love God as she loved God.

> *If we are faithful to the Lord's church, mother can get a witness.*
>
> *If we stand on God's word, Mother can get a witness.*
>
> *If we nurture our spirits in songs of praise, Mother can get a witness.*
>
> *If we know Jesus for ourselves, Mother can get a witness.*
>
> *If we go where the Lord wants us to go, Mother can get a witness.*
>
> *If we do what the Lord wants us to do, Mother can get a witness.*
>
> *If we praise God, who is worthy of all praise, Mother can get a witness.*
>
> *Can mother get a witness?*

THE DAY WHEN MOTHER LAUGHS AT GOD

Text: *They said to him, "Where is Sarah your wife?" And he said, "She is in the tent." The Lord said, "I will surely return to you in the spring, and Sarah your wife shall have a son." And Sarah was listening at the tent door behind him. Now Abraham and Sarah were old, advanced in age; it had ceased to be with Sarah after the manner of women. So Sarah laughed to herself, saying, "After I have grown old, and my husband is old, shall I have pleasure?" The Lord said to Abraham, "Why did Sarah laugh, and say, 'Shall I indeed bear a child, now that I am old?' Is anything too hard for the Lord? At the appointed time I will return to you, in the spring, and Sarah shall have a son." But Sarah denied saying, "I did not laugh"; for she was afraid. He said, "No, but you did laugh."* (**Genesis 18:9-15**, RSV)

It has been often stated that "there is no love like a mother's love." Such a positive statement must hinge upon the faithful promise that mother has for her children. A measure of creative optimism must surely shape such a warm assessment of mothering. A mother's love seems to rest upon the assumption that Mother loves mothering. One must see a glowing hope, a faithful future, a positive pilgrimage in the task of mothering.

As the story of Abraham and Sarah dramatically unfolds, we are almost caught off balance by their dogged determination to be blessed with a child. God had repeatedly assured them of descendants that would leap from their faith. In many and sundry ways God expounded upon His promise. However, the impatient yearnings of Sarah and Abraham found ways of intervening in God's promised pronouncements. Abraham entered into pact with his servant, Eliezer. Sarah arranged a surrogate experience with her servant, Hagar.

How often is it that we attempt to rush God's blessings

upon ourselves? In our impatient gropings, we often do more blundering than blessing. God is no stranger to human impatience. But God will still only bless in His own time.

Frustration foiled every impatient act on the part of Abraham and Sarah to bless themselves. Nonetheless, in God's own time the message comes to Abraham, "your wife, Sarah, shall have a son." Abraham and Sarah are old, advanced in years. The years had piled upon each of their frames. As the Lord spoke to Abraham, Sarah overheard and broke out in laughter.

Is it not interesting how God speaks? God spoke to one, but all who were faithfully involved were blessed to hear. If you have ears to hear, you ought to hear what thus says the Lord. God's speaking is not for individuals alone, but for everyone concerned. God may speak to a husband, but the wife ought to hear something. God may speak to the wife, but the husband ought to hear something. God may speak specifically to the preacher-pastor, but the congregation ought to hear something. God may speak to the prophet, but the nation ought to hear. God's words and blessings are for all who hear and receive. If you have a role to play in the blessings of God, you ought to hear something.

God spoke to Abraham, but Sarah was blessed to hear. Sarah responded to what she heard by laughing to herself. She laughed at what she heard from the Lord. With gut-busting humor, she asked, "After I have grown old, and my husband is old, shall I have pleasure?" Unlike the sexual pleasure-seekers of our day, the ancients viewed child bearing as pleasurable. One never heard what we currently hear, such as, "Having babies is the pits." Or, "raising children is for the dogs." Another crowd boldly proclaims, "I ain't having any children for no one." The ancient Hebrews (and Africans) saw childbearing as a blessing from

God. Children promised a future. Children offered hope for the unvisited tomorrows. Children tied up and wrapped up the divine plan and pilgrimage. Where there were no children, the future was doubtful. Children were reasons for pleasure. The daybreak of tomorrow rested on the hope of children.

Sarah laughed because she saw no possibility for children. Many of us know well the story of Abraham and Sarah. We know how they left all at the beckoning of God. Their destiny was unknown to them, for God had not revealed the "where" of their journey. God only revealed the "what" of their journey. Where they were headed was unknown, but what to expect was clearly stated. A land of familiarity was abandoned for the unknown. **"Go from your country and kindred and your father's house to the land that I will show you,"** said the Lord. Centuries later someone wrote the awesome words, **"By faith Abraham obeyed when he was called to go out to a place which he was to receive...."** Abraham and Sarah left all to go with God.

Faith still has much to do with the unexpected **"the substance of things hoped for and the evidence of things not seen."** Faith still has much to do with the mysterious. Someone said, "Faith never knows where it is being led, but it knows the One who is leading." Sarah and Abraham went out on the scandalous wings of faith. Faith is not a reasonable act which fits into the normal scheme of things. Faith can be totally unreasonable.

Having never been a mother and never will, nonetheless,I risk making a judgment. I want to posit the notion that Mothering is an act of faith. To be a mother is to engage in a faith pilgrimage. That's why there is no love like a mother's love. Mother's love is not just love, it's faith. Mothering, from conception on, is a whole lot of the unexpected. In our days of growing single-parenting, and widespread absentee fathers, mothers face the unknown. Mothering deals with the mysterious. No mother assuredly knows what her children might become. Mothers live by faith. **"The substance of things hoped for and the evidence of things not seen."**

The child may be successful, but the child may just as well be a failure. The child may come to court as a lawyer, or be in court as a criminal. The child may be in the hospital as a doctor, or the child may lie in the hospital as a victim of a Saturday night shoot-out. The child may work the streets as a civic leader, or the child may walk the streets as a gangster, a whore, a drug addict, or an alcoholic. Mother never knows. The child may prove faithful or foolish, generous or greedy, selfless or selfish, mean or kind. Mothers mother in faith. They really **"walk by faith and not by sight."**

Sarah looked at herself, counted her years, and reminisced on what used to be a human possibility. She laughed at herself, but in reality she laughed at God. In her estimation, according to her calculation, Mothering was out! Her womb had been closed and the years had rusted her desire. To make matters worse, not only was she old, but so was her husband. Her laughter grew from the question, "How in the world can two old folk work this out?"

Barrenness was taken seriously. Sarah's barrenness was the solemn signal of being without a future. Since Sarah could bear no children, she believed herself to have failed her husband and life. The future was dismal. The tomorrows were dark. A barren woman was the least among many and considered cursed by all. Sarah laughed at her barrenness.

I suppose there are countless mothers, who often feel like Sarah. Although blessed with child and sometimes children, women are laughing because the fruit of their wombs has gone astray. Countless mothers see children who offer no hope. All of their mothering seems to have been in vain. "For what cause, O Lord, did this child come into the world?" they ask. "My child produces nothing but one heartache after another. Disappointments follow disappointments." Her blessings are curses. Her joys are sorrows.

Barren is the mother when all of her children prefer to sink to the bottom of life. The reason so many parents are raising grandchildren is because of fruitless sons and daughters. Mothers are looking to their grandchildren for a spark of a bright future. Mothers are laughing to keep from crying.

The church, as the bride of Christ, the spiritual womb of a new world order, also seems to be laughing. Like Sarah, whose laughing expressed a disbelief in God, the church seems to be laughing. We have heard of all that God has promised us and commanded of us. Yet, we look at our feebled bodies, chilly spirits, mean hearts, and stingy hands. We laugh because we do not see how God can bless us to give birth to new world order. How can the kingdom come through people with so many deficits?

Our own children are falling through the cracks of despair. We laugh when they do something cute, and even when they stumble into disaster. We laugh like Sarah, who somehow forgot she was a part of God's promise and purpose. We laugh at the troubles of the world, as if the world offers no hope for tomorrow. We laugh at sin when we should be crying. Has not God called us to prepare a church without spot or wrinkle? Has not God called us to be a priesthood of believers, a household of faith? How can we laugh, when giving birth to a new world order is ours to perform?

It is a sad day when Mother laughs at God. Sarah laughed! And the Lord said to Abraham, **"Why did Sarah laugh? Is there anything too hard for the Lord?"** The Bible says that Sarah laughed because she was afraid. The Lord suggested that fear and faith can not occupy the same temple. Fear drains away faith. Fear is a contradiction of faith. Sarah laughed because she was afraid.

Mothers, it may be that the sins of the time are so cruel and awesome that fear has become unavoidable. Maybe mother is laughing because she is really afraid of what harm this mean world will bring upon a child. Mother is afraid of the darkness of our nights. Mother is afraid of the evil in sight. Mother is afraid of the wickedness of our paths,and the traps set therein. Mother is afraid of the deadly grip of death and despair. The future for African American children can look bleak, if not impossible. But there is a word of hope. Jesus said, **"Be of good cheer; I have overcome the world."**

"Is there anything too hard for the Lord?" The word "hard" in the Hebrew also means "wonderful." In other words, the Lord is asking us: "Is anything, any impossible circumstance, any human circumstance, too wonderful for the Lord?" The story is that God blessed Sarah in spite of her years, in spite of her disbelief, in spite of barren circumstances. God blessed her to be a mother. Her son's name was Isaac, which means "God has laughed, or God has smiled."

Mothers, there is nothing too wonderful for the Lord. The going may seem tough, the road may seem rough; the hills high and the valleys low. The good news of Jesus is God has smiled on you. Jesus brings to our situations the smile of God. He brings new life to our barren situations. He adds joy to our circumstances. God has smiled on you.

God is wonderful! God gives birth to barrenness.

God is wonderful! God gives a powerful future to a pitiful present.

God is wonderful! God blesses the blundering.

God is wonderful! God calls back home the prodigal.

God is wonderful! God seeks out the wandering.

God is wonderful! God saves the lost and gives sight to the blind.

God is wonderful! God dries up the drunk and cleanses the drugged.

God is wonderful! For even on a dark Friday, while nailed to a cross, God gives a mourning mother a son and a lonesome son a mother.

God is wonderful! Hallelujah! Hallelujah! Praise God!

PRAYING MOTHER, BELIEVING MOTHER, REJOICING MOTHER

Text: *"And she was in bitterness of soul, and prayed to the Lord and wept in anguish. Then she made a vow and said, "O, Lord of hosts, if You will indeed look on the affliction of your maidservant and remember me, and not forget your maidservant, but will give your maidservant a male child, then I will give him to the Lord all the days of his life, and no razor shall come upon his head." And it happened, as she continued praying before the Lord, that Eli watched her mouth. Now Hannah spoke in her heart; only her lips moved, but her voice was not heard. Therefore, Eli thought she was drunk. So Eli said to her, "How long will you be drunk? Put your wine away from you!" And Hannah answered and said, "No, my Lord, I am a woman of sorrowful spirit. I have drunk neither wine nor intoxicating drink, but have poured out my soul before the Lord. Do not consider your maidservant a wicked woman, for out of the abundance of my complaint and grief I have spoken until now." Then Eli answered and said, "Go in peace, and the God of Israel grant your petition which you have asked of Him." And she said, "Let your maidservant find favor in your sight." So the woman went her way and ate, and her face was no longer sad. And Hannah prayed and said: "My heart rejoices in the Lord; My horn is exalted in the Lord. I smile at my enemies, Because I rejoice in Your salvation. There is none holy like the Lord, For there is none besides You, Nor is there any rock like our God. Talk no more so very proudly; Let no arrogance come from your mouth, for the Lord is the God of knowledge; And by Him actions are weighed. The bows of the mighty men are broken, And those who stumbled are girded with strength. Those who were full have hired themselves out for bread, And those who were hungry have ceased to hunger. Even the barren has borne seven, And she who has many children has become feeble. The Lord kills and makes alive; He brings down to the grave and brings up. The Lord makes poor and makes rich; He brings low and lifts up. He raises the poor from the dust and lifts the beggar from the ash heap, To set them among princes and make them inherit the throne of glory.*

For the pillars of the earth are the Lord's, And He has set the world upon them. He will guard the feet of His saints, But the wicked shall be silent in darkness. For by strength no man shall prevail. The adversaries of the Lord shall be broken in pieces; From heaven He will thunder against them. The Lord will judge the ends of the earth. He will give strength to His king, And exalt the horn of His anointed. (**I Samuel 1:10-18; 2:1-10**, New King James Version)

The desires and struggle of motherhood are as ancient as time itself. Mothering lifts ordinary people onto the stage of extraordinary events. History is full of celebrated personalities who footnote their achievements with the struggles of a mother. Heros and heroines hold that Mother behaved in such a way as to guide them into success. Many are the features of celebrated motherhood, but the character of our text lifts up certain features that are noteworthy and attainable. I hold that the difficulties of mothering African American children could be profoundly affected by these Hannanian features.

One of the clearest features evident in the narrative picture of Hannah is the fact that she was a praying woman. She understood that the key to meaningful life would be found through prayer. Prayer was the primary instrument used by Hannah to set in bright light the dark mysteries of life. Hannah knew that if life was worth living its worth would be discovered through prayer. As a result we feature Hannah in prayer.

It would do us well to note that Hannah prayed before she became a mother, while she was a mother, and after she surrendered her child into the service of the Lord. In other words, she prayed before she ever had a child at home. She prayed while the child was at home. And she prayed after the child left home. She was a praying mother throughout the totality of her motherhood experiences.

I suspect that the number of unwanted children would

not be so incredibly high, if we had more mothers praying prior to giving birth. If many of our young women were practitioners of prayer, instead of samplers of sex, we would not have children suffering because of the mistakes of immaturity. Our young women need to listen more for divine directions rather than biologically motivated gibberish. God has more to say to our young women than some young, cool, immature brother. Young Sisters, God knows how to say what needs to be said better than some slick talking gigolo. However, there needs to be some praying going on before you get too far gone, or you will find yourself all alone.

Even young married persons and expectant parents need to engage themselves in sincere prayer before bringing a child into this crazy, mixed-up world. We are expecting our first child. We have been busy preparing ourselves for our child's entrance into the world. We have read some. (Karen has read everything.) We have talked with people (Karen has talked to everybody). We have attended classes and will be viewing movies and practicing breathing exercises. I plan to be in the delivery room, scrubbed down, during the delivery. Yet prior to all of our preparation, we went to the Lord in prayer. Moreover, I have not stopped praying. I want the Lord to make me the kind of parent that God wants me to be. I not only want God to make me a good parent when the child comes here, I want God to start working on me before the child ever gets here. I know if I, as a potential father, sense a need to pray, I suspect mothers need to pray the more. Hannah prayed before the child's conception and birth.

She not only prayed before the child's birth, but she prayed while the child was in her care. We have heard numerous testimonies of mothers who pray for the children in their immediate care. Children have a way of producing praying mothers. If the child is going bad and headed toward self-destruction, mother is praying. If the child is doing good and life opens wide the gates of bless- edness, mother is praying. If it seems that life is giving a child one bad break after another, mother is praying. If no cruel obstacles hinder the child's progress, mother is praying.

The Black mother holds a unique place in the history of motherhood. She has had to demonstrate an indomi- table spirit in the face of awesome odds. She has been raped and misused by the senseless passions of a racist so- ciety. She has had to watch heartbroken as her children have been sold, whipped, brutalized, homosexualized, jailed and murdered. She has often had to raise a house full of children, while society denied her husband the right to re- sponsible fatherhood. She raised white folk's children, cleaned their houses, while her own children were home alone making it the best way they could. Black mothers still wear the scars of a brutal wound inflicted by an uncar- ing white man's world, and a misunderstanding Black com- munity. Yet, Black mothers have held on.

If there is any one reason to explain her ability to hold on, it is because mother has been praying. If any one source is responsible for her holding on power, it has been the power of prayer. Mother has been praying and mother is still praying, and mother will always be praying. Pray on, Black mother! Pray on!

Hannah prayed while Samuel was at home, but she also prayed when he left home. I am not a mother, and I never will be. However, I sense that the praying mother contin- ues to pray when the child leaves home. The reason I sense the presence of continued prayers from mother is because it has been so real with me. I used to run the streets all night long, sometimes for days at a time. I knew what I was doing was far from right, but I felt I could get away with it because mother was praying for me. I know that may sound odd, but if the truth be told, we are often guilty of exploiting prayers.

Nonetheless, as I continued to run rampant and my time ticked slim, God saved me and brought me into the newness of life. Shortly after I was converted I looked into my mother's face. She did not have to say a word, for I knew that mother had been praying for me. In the parable of the "prodigal son," there is mention only about a father and two sons. However, I know that a mother was praying behind the scenes. I used good sense, not imagination, to picture the presence of a mother humming over pots and pans. Mother was praying for her pig-pen son, in a far country. Oh, yes! She was there. She had to be there because she has always been there for you and me. While we were in the house and while we were out of the house, mother prayed and she prays. Pray on, mother! Pray on!

Hannah prayed when her child left home to be in the service of the Lord. A child does not necessarily have to be a preacher to be in the service of the Lord. A child does not have to be a male-child to be in the service of the Lord. Whatever the child, male or female, finds in life to do, it should be done swiftly and well; such service is what God has chosen for you. If for no other reason we complete our task, let us do it because mother asked. The day hopefully will come when we can sing "My Mother's Prayer".

> *I never can forget the day*
> *I heard my mother kindly say,*
> *"You're leaving my tender care*
> *Remember, child, your mother's prayer."*

Hannah was not only a praying mother, she was a believing mother. For some time I have been arguing against the prevailing negrological theology that "Prayer changes things." I think now that I have discovered biblical evidence to support my claim. If we look closely at the text, we find not the thing that disturbed Hannah being changed. But we find Hannah being changed. The obstacle remained. Hannah changed.

Things do not need to change; it is people who need to change. We need to change our limited views of life and look beyond our narrow perspectives. We need to change our feeble minds and share in some cosmological thinking with God. God is big and God acts in big ways. We need to ask God, "Don't move the mountain, just give me the strength to climb." Let us be like David and not ask for leveled valleys, but say, "even though I walk through the valley in the very shadows of death I will be all right, because your rod and staff comfort me." Since God is in our prayers, we can change.

I believe that the reason we find mothers so apt to pray is that they believe in prayer. Mothers must believe to maintain such a vigil in prayer. Prayer must not be perceived as an instrument for selfish manipulation. Prayers are signals of belief. Mothers are not out to "jive" God. There is sincere belief before the prayer is uttered. When mother goes down in prayer, she is actually going up to the altar of God.

I know that Black mothers have had, and still have, an unfaltering belief in God. Such a belief fueled mothers to believe that we would be free one day. During our slavery experience, mothers would comfort one another after watching families being savagely destroyed. Mother would sing to mother, "Oh Mary don't you weep, tell Martha not to moan. Ol' Pharoah got drowned in the sea one day."

What they were actually saying through the symbolic language of belief was, " you can sell our children and deny our men their manhood; but we believe that there is a God who will provide a way through the Red Seas of oppression." Mother believed that we would overcome. Mother believed. Believe on, Mother! Believe on!

Mothers believe that no matter how hard the journey there will be smooth sailing one day. Mothers believe that no matter how dark the night may seem, there is a bright side somewhere. One of the great poets of our race, Langston Hughes, was moved by the belief of his mother. One day he dipped his poetic pen in the belief system of his mother and wrote memorable words:

> Well, son, I'll tell you;
> Life for me ain't been no crystal stair
> It's had tacks in it,
> And splinters
> And boards torn up,
> And places with no carpet on the floor—Bare.
> But all the time
> I'se been a-climbin' on
> And turnin' corners,
> And sometimes goin' in the dark
> Where there ain't been no light—
> So boy, don't you turn back.
> Don't you set down on the steps
> 'Cause you finds it's kinder hard,
> Don't you fall now—
> For I'se still going honey,
> I'se still climbin'
> And life for me ain't been no crystal stair.

When Samuel had been taken to the temple to begin his great service for the Lord, Hannah's prayer climaxed in rejoicing. Hannah prayed. Hannah believed. Hannah rejoiced. Why did Hannah rejoice? How could she rejoice when her recently weaned, only son was leaving home for good? Mothers do not usually rejoice under such circumstances. But in the contents of Hannah's prayer we find her reasons for rejoicing.

It seems that Hannah had never interpreted her child to be her child only. There rings from her joyous utterances an awareness that her child was God's child. She appears to know that her child would not and could not be limited to the maternal fondling of her household. The child was to be used of God.

Oh, how many mothers care to see their children used in the service of his/her people, as a servant of the Lord? Mothers can usually deal with the idea of children belonging to God (some can and some can't). But many mothers find it difficult accepting their children being used by the people. Such a situation is hard for mother to deal with. Yet if we do not deal with it, we will never reverse the destructive cycle of our people.

We need to get away from shaping our children to be like us, as masseuses of our egos. Our children need to be shaped and formed for service to God, as they serve humanity. We have too many wet-head Mamma's boys in our communities. Their value system has been so warped that they now overcrowd the penal systems. We don't need any mamma's boys to spoil our people, we need strong men to build up our people. We don't need any confused Daddy's girls to continuously confuse our progeny. No! Babies cannot adequately raise babies. We need responsible mothers to wean our children to be keepers of our people. Our children need to be worth more to society than a good reason to build bigger and better jails, and to pad the welfare roll.

Hannah rejoiced because she understood that her child would do great things for God's people. She understood that her child's destiny was tied up in the destiny of the people. She rejoiced because purpose was being fulfilled.

I want to believe, today, that our mothers will have reason to rejoice. I want to believe that Black mothers can discover reasons to rejoice. Rejoice like Hannah, who said, "My heart rejoiceth in the Lord. My heart rejoices because my child will play a role in the drama of redemption. My heart rejoices because God has included my child in the salvation of God's people. My heart rejoices because God used me in His plan." Our mothers need to rejoice.

Look at Mother Mary! She, too, rejoiced. She said,

"My soul doth magnify the Lord."

My child will be talked about, but that's all right. My soul doth magnify the Lord."

My child will make me cry sometime, but that's all right. "My soul doth magnify the Lord."

My child will give me some sleepless nights, but that's all right. "My soul doth magnify the Lord."

They are going to nail my child on an Old Rugged Cross, but that's all right. "My soul doth magnify the Lord."

They will stretch him wide and hang him high, but that's all right. "My soul doth magnify the Lord."

I don't know about you, but I have brought tears to my mother's eyes. I have caused her some sleepless nights. I know we have moments of misunderstanding. Yet, I pray that for the balance of her days she can join Mary and Hannah and sing: "My soul doth magnify the Lord."

DELIVERING THE BLACK FATHER
FROM EXILE

Text: *"Most men will proclaim each his own goodness, but who can find a faithful man." (**Proverbs 20:6,** New King James Version)*

Israel's genius to the religious world can never be discounted. No matter what we may think of "Jews," their contribution to religion is inestimable. Why even in exile, words of faith and wisdom were issued forth. The words of our text were possibly composed out of the painful experience of being out of relationship with their homeland. Unable to defend the homefront, because they were not at home, they pondered over the deep meanings of life. "Most men will proclaim each his own goodness, but who can find a faithful man?"

Interestingly enough these words sound so familiar. A lot of brothers declare how good they are, how noble their intentions, how good their hearts. Yet, the question being raised throughout the Black community is: who can find a faithful man?

One of the most disturbing crises of Black family life is that the majority of our households are without the influence of the Black father. Most Black children are being raised by mothers only. Another way of putting it is for every three Black children being born two will spend much of their lives wondering, "Where is my father?" Most will not only wonder "where is my father?" but "who is my father?" We are presently trying to pull off the impossible feat of trying to sustain a race without the benefits of both parents. We have seemingly surrendered to some Amazonian myth that women, alone, can save our race.

Fathering represents the greatest accomplishment of manhood. The man who parents his children serves as a

God-appointed co-agent for the salvation of the world. A father represents an invaluable resource in shaping human personality. The father is the set-up man for a child's understanding of the world. The father blesses a home, stabilizes the family, dignifies a mother, and sanctifies a child. A father is indispensable to the health of the human race, particularly the African American race. In this culture, father has been portrayed as God's representative in the home. However, someone has replied, "A child is not likely to find a father in God unless he finds something of God in his father."

Black people can not get too comfortable with the present parental arrangements of our families. God never intended for our families to be single-parent, mother-led phenomena. Our families are at their best when father does his best. It is not that father knows best, it is about father doing what is best for his family. Black fathers are most needed and more effective when they occupy the homefront. African American families need in-the-trenches, front-line, home-front, kind-of-men. The influence of fatherly presence depends upon the father being present.

The strategy of evil has always been to place the father in some exile, away from the homefront. A father in exile destroys the homefront. Exile takes place when people are removed from their natural environment. To be in exile is to live away from the place where one is supposed to live. Exilic living is the painful attempt to carve out an existence in alien and hostile territory. Exile can be forced, or it can be voluntary. People are forced into exile, or they willingly go into exile.

The Black father is clearly outside of his native environment, when he is living without his family. A father away from the homefront is a father not where he is supposed to be. The comforts of life will not cushion the pain of living in alien territory. No thinking person can deny that the racist evils of American society have enforced family exile upon many Black fathers. Unemployment is a forced exile. Being discriminated against is a forced exile. I had a senior sister tell of a white man who dated a married black woman in the presence of her black husband and he could not do anything about it. Society was so arranged that he was in exile. Impatient, misunderstanding, insensitive Black women can assist a forced exile. A non-supportive, always competing brotherhood can also aid and abet a forced exile.

But when males make babies and don't care for them, that is a voluntary exile. To allow the misunderstandings of former spouses to make you irresponsible to your children, that is a voluntary exile. To place distance between you and your children is voluntary exile. To create reasons not to do, what you know you should do, is a voluntary exile. To fall in love with a woman, other than your wife, is a voluntary exile. To emotionally detach yourself from the hearts, hands, and lives of your children, that is a voluntary exile. We carve out exilic lives when we remove ourselves from the homefront.

In his book, <u>Point Man</u>, Steve Farr points out that the devil's strategy to destroy humanity is to destroy the family. Farr asserts that the devil can more easily destroy the family when he can remove the influence of the man from the family. A man-less family is easy prey for the devil. If the devil can do two things, he will have easy access to the family. First of all, if he can alienate and sever the ties between the man and the woman, he will destroy the human race. Secondly, if he can alienate and sever the ties between a man and his children, he will certainly destroy the family. Sisters, I recognize your strong feelings about your competency as a mother. But God never intended for you to fight the devil by yourself. No woman can adequately raise children by herself. God did not make women to be mothers and fathers. Such thinking is fantasy at best, and foolishness at its worst. Might I also add no woman can adequately raise a boy to be a man. It takes a man to make a boy a man. Moreover, it takes a Black man to make a Black boy to be a Black man in white America.

The task of our race is to deliver the black man from exile to save our race. The words of our text lead us in the direction of delivering Black men from exile. **"Most men will proclaim each his own goodness, but who can find a good man?"** The observation of the text notices that men see within themselves fatherly potential. "Most men will proclaim their own goodness...." Brethren, we see within ourselves the potential to be what God intends for us to be. We see our potential even when we are in exile. Men can be ever so in left field, but can see themselves making it home. The very fact that men see themselves being good men suggests that fatherhood is possible. The challenge for us, my brethren, is to move beyond talk. We must stop talking about ourselves and start becoming ourselves. God wants us to become faithful fathers. God wants us to return to the homefront and recover our families. Exile is always temporary, home is permanent. God wants us in our permanent places.

Who can find a faithful man? The word "faithful" has a "homey" meaning in the original language. It suggests more than a single-eyed affection to one woman. Faithfulness literally means "to be established." A faithful man is an established man, a man who has a permanent place. A faithful man is not a man of exile, a man out of place. It is a man who knows his place, has his place, and holds his place.

Deliverance from exile requires that a man be established. Fatherhood means to be established. If we are to be delivered from the places of our exile, we must estab-

lish ourselves in our homes. The first place to be established is in the heart of our children's mother. Some of you
may be divorced, but a divorce does not mean it is impossible for your children's mother to trust you. So many of
us have never established a place in the heart of our
children's mother. The most lasting impression on a child
that a father can make is how he treats the child's mother.
The relationship patterns of our children's lives are largely
determined by how the child's parents relate. I am presently reading a book entitled, <u>Cool Pose</u>. This book represents the first study of the "cool" phenomenon of Black
males. The proposition is that Black men become cool in
response to a society that offers a dream to everybody but
him. Coolness is a socio-spiritual response to the denials
of racism. It is a form of psychological anesthesia from
the pain of social denial. Coolness has enabled Black men
to survive, būt it has also made meaningful relationships
impossible. We are cool enough to get our woman, but
too cool to keep our women. We are too cool to get close
to our own women. Our children need to see us warming
up to their mother, being real, intimate, and affectionate.

Secondly, deliverance from exile requires that we become established in the hearts of our children. Our children need fathers' touch to begin at the rocking of the cradle.
I can recall my own childhood. The only time I was ever
excited about seeing Daddy come home was when we were
going fishing. Daddy's arrival generally never created any
excitement. Daddy was always aloof, distant, and objective. There was nothing subjectively attractive about
Daddy. Daddy essentially represented two things: work
or a whipping. He either wanted to work me, or whip me.
Either I had to do something, or I was being reprimanded
for leaving undone what I was supposed to do. I praise
God that Daddy and I are much closer now. We call one

another several times in a month. But during my childhood, there was nothing exciting about Daddy coming home.

Many call my children bad, spoiled, and probably some other things. I call them my children. They are always glad to see me. They run with joy, almost knocking me off my feet, whenever I come home. I receive this treatment at the end of a day, or at the end of a trip. They are always glad to see me. As soon as church is dismissed, no one gets to me as quickly as my children. There is some excitement in our relationship, and I love every bit of it. It is not always convenient, but I always love it. God has had to work on me to deliver me from being emotionally exiled from my children. God had to get me to leave the emotional coolness of my past and cleave to the unity of another vision of family. I know I still have a long way to go, but God is still working on me. I want to be established in the hearts of my children. I do not want a teenager to teach my child sex education, race relations, or how to love yourself. NO teacher is responsible for my children's education. The preacher is not responsible for my child's religious formation. I am the professor of life for those children. I am the established professor of "A to Z," "Birds and Bees," "love you—love me," as well as God said, "let there be." Fatherhood requires being established in the hearts of our children.

Finally, deliverance from exile demands that a father be established in the heart of God. The text says, **"Most men will proclaim each his own goodness, but who can find a faithful man?"** There was once a confrontation between one man and another man. One man called the other good. The other man responded, **"Call no man good. There is none good, but God."** Men will discover the measure of their own goodness when they establish themselves in the heart of God. Notice, I say in the heart of God not God in our hearts.

Many of our popular songs have reduced God to human heart size. We sing, "In my heart" and "Jesus in my heart," and "He lives within my heart." The truth is God is most God when we are established in the heart of God. God's heart is truly a good heart. Once established in God's heart, we can be more of what God intends for us to be.

God's heart is more loving, which means we can be more loving.

God's heart is wise, which means we can be more wise.

God's heart is patient, which means we can be more patient.

God's heart is understanding, which means we can be more understanding.

God's heart is forgiving, which means we can bring more forgiveness into our families.

God's heart is warm, which means we can be more warm.

God's heart is truly faithful, which means we can be faithful men.

Most of all, God can always be found. God is never in exile. God is always where God is supposed to be. Someone said, "He is nearer than breathing; nearer than hands and feet." God is always wherever we need God the most, which means we can call upon God. God is always near.

God is always at home.

"Come and go with me to my Father's house.

There is joy, in my Father's house.

There is peace, in my Father's house.

Come and go with me to my Father's house."

HEALING FOR THE BLACK FAMILY MAN

Text: *"And He entered the synagogue again, and a man was there who had a withered hand. And they watched Him closely, whether He would heal him on the Sabbath, so that they might accuse Him. Then He said to the man who had the withered hand, "Step forward." And He said to them, 'Is it lawful on the Sabbath to do good or to do evil, to save life or to kill?' But they kept silent. So when He had looked around at their anger, being grieved by the hardness of their hearts, He said to the man, 'Stretch out your hand.' And he stretched it out, and his hand was restored as whole as the other. Then the Pharisees went out and immediately plotted with the Herodians against Him, how they might destroy Him."* **Mark 3:1-6** (New King James Version)

If we adults really knew how much attention children give to our words and deeds, we would be most careful in all that we do and everything that we say. I recall, as a young boy, a piece of advice that spread throughout our family. I even recall who first spoke those words of advice in my hearing. My grandfather, Mack Miles, "Big Daddy" we called him, advised us that we should never drink milk and eat fish at the same time.

Big Daddy was not a doctor, a biochemist, or even a dietician. He had never attended medical school, and as far as I know He had never worked around a hospital. Big Daddy was a farmer who migrated to the city and tried to make it in a factory. But, when Big Daddy advised that no one should ever eat fish and drink milk at the same time, all of the family took heed. There were six girls and two boys, most of them were married and had children. When I heard Big Daddy's words, I sensed that the children, in-laws, and all of the grandchildren took heed to his words. I would even risk saying that I doubt that any of us have ever eaten fish and drunk milk at the same time. Big Daddy has been in his grave over twenty-years, but the powerful male image he gave to our family lives on.

I raise up Big Daddy's admonition not to discourage eating fish and drinking milk (although I doubt that I will ever indulge); but I lift up Big Daddy as an example of a powerful Black family man. The point is on whatever issue Big Daddy gave voice and opinion, the entire family fell in line. His moving presence even carried over into the Saint John Missionary Baptist Church, where he served as a deacon. Whenever Deacon Mack Miles spoke, the whole church would give ear. Even now some of the senior members of the church are living off of his words.

Something evil and sick has eroded our families, since the Big Daddies of yesteryear faded off the scene. A terrifying void has been left by the absence of strong Black family men. Our Big Daddies have been tragically replaced with "Sugar Daddies" and "Little Daddies." Most of our families don't even know what it means to have a male presence, let alone male power. And where there is a male presence, he rarely possesses any real power. I know men who will not even speak, because they know they will not be heard. Many of us will be lucky to get the dog's attention, let alone the members of our families. How many families can you name where a Black male can speak and everybody falls in line? Is there any wonder, then, why black men lack real power in the church?

I speak not of positions. Any one can hold some of these male-dominated positions. Positions are no guarantee of power. The power I refer to is that spiritual depth and moral fortitude that commands and demands respect and admiration. I refer to positive influence over minds that has the well-being of the other at heart. Power has to do with the capacity to act in a responsible manner which clearly indicates that one is in tune with the will of God. Such power comes from faithfulness to God and not solely from the election of people.

As I prayerfully waited on God to guide me in this sermon struggle, God steered me to ponder today's text. At first I did not understand how a man with a withered hand could give insight on the Black family man. But, as I prayed, listened, and studied God's direction was sure. The story finds Jesus entering again into the synagogue. His first entrance into the synagogue, Chapter 1, placed him before a man with a withered spirit. Jesus' teaching proved powerful enough to deliver the man from the evil spirit. Jesus left the synagogue and went directly to Peter's house, where Peter's mother-in-law was sick with a fever. I strongly believe that the demon in the church house was related to the fever in Peter's house. Nonetheless, Jesus' second entrance into the synagogue brought Him in contact with the man with a withered hand.

Like the demon-possessed man of Chapter 1, there in God's house was a man so spiritually, emotionally, physically, and socially deformed that he lacked the power to do any of the things a man should do. He is described as having a withered hand. The hand, according to scripture, nearly always refers to power. "Jesus sits at the right hand of God." "The hand of the Lord was upon him...." " God delivered us out of the hand of the Egyptians." "All power in heaven and earth is in his hand."

A man's hand represented the power of a man, or a man's capacity to act. In the Gospel of the Hebrews, an apocryphal writing, the man of our text is identified as a brick mason who had become incapacitated. He was unable to perform his task. The word "withered" is the same word use as the "withered tree," a tree unable to produce, or perform, as a tree ought to perform. The man, with the withered hand, was a powerless man. He was an unproductive man, an irresponsible man. He could not hug his wife, nor play with his children. He lacked the capacity to give a gentle touch; to work, or to pray with outstretched hands. He was a man out of whose life God received no glory.

As we ponder the plight of the Black family, placing it under the microscope of spiritual scrutiny, a diagnosis can be offered. Certainly the Black family is hurting. Its illnesses are legion. The Black family is weak and fragile. But, what is really wrong with the Black family? One thing we must say, as painful as it is, the weakness of the Black family can be diagnosed as a weakness in the presence and power of the Black male. In other words, the Black man is like a man with a withered hand.

Please, don't be hard on us. We have not always been like this. We once were builders, like the man of our text. We once were the world's greatest architects. We once built civilizations, carved highways in the desert, and built castles in the sand. We are the world's oldest practitioners of medical science and mortuary science. We once built nations and fully aligned our lives to the will of God. Black men have been creative and inventive.

We need to consider that it is not easy getting well after three hundred years of slavery. Please don't expect us to get well overnight after one hundred years of Jim Crow segregation, and less than thirty years of improved civil rights. We are still suffering from having our history erased, our names changed, our language taken away, our family structures destroyed, and our manhood obliterated. There are some undeniable historical reasons, some social causes, and some political and economical forces that continue to conspire to keep our hands withered.

We are not asking for sympathy. Yet, the Black family man's presence and power has been undermined by the most wicked of strategies. Our women are taught not to believe in us, not to trust us, and to despise us. Our children are taught to disrespect us and disobey us. Someone has said, "The Black male on a day-to-day basis finds himself in an insecure and hostile world where his presence commands little, if any respect; where his marketability as worker and provider is slowly eroded by unemployment and hyper-inflation; and where his association with Black women and children is often frustrating and non-developing."

It doesn't matter what you drive in, where you live, what you wear, or how you look; if a man lacks power and presence in the family he is a man with a withered hand. But, thank God for Jesus. Jesus comes to us apart from any racist portrayal of Him. He shows up for us, where we are, to address our deepest needs. Jesus yet heals and makes whole. He is still giving power to the weak and to those without might He increases strength. There is healing for the Black family man.

Notice where Jesus goes and finds the withered hand man. Also, notice the resistance of the powers that be. Jesus went to the synagogue. For the Christian, Jesus embodies Himself in the presence of believers. The presence of the church, not buildings, but the people of God offer healing for the Black family man. A senior pastor noted that the Black community has more buildings than churches. Yet, Jesus is most known among His people.

Jesus' presence among God's people, however, caused a negative response. There were those who were watching to see if Jesus would break the rules of the Sabbath. In reality, there was no way for the Lord of the Sabbath to violate the rules of the Sabbath. In fact, God needs no rules to meet our needs. People's needs are more important than rules. But, it is always strange that whenever someone seeks to help Blacks, the rules always change. Whenever healing for Black men is imminent, the rules always change. As soon as we began taking advantage of affirmative action, the rules changed. When it becomes less difficult for us to gain a quality education, the rules change with propositions and depositions. When it appeared that the Black man might be healed, George Bush vetoed the Civil Rights bill and started a war, with our people disproportionately on the front line. The rules always change when time comes for our healing.

Yet, it doesn't matter when Jesus is concerned. Jesus comes along and breaks the rules. Men say one thing, God says something else. The powers plot, but Jesus performs. Just like the man with the withered hand, Jesus is available to heal the Black family man. If we follow the example of the man with the withered hand we could experience healing for the Black family man. There are three steps toward wholeness, power and presence. Jesus called the man to first, "stand up." Brethren, for us to be healed as men with capacity to act, we will have to stand up. Let us stand up, withered hand and all. Quit trying to fake as if nothing is wrong with us. Stop trying to hide our collective weaknesses. When Jesus calls, it is all right to stand up. Standing up is an act of anticipation. Standing registers a strong belief that something is about to happen.

Let us stand up and show the world, yes, "I have a withered hand. Yes, I have not been able to act as I should act. Yes, I have not demonstrated power in my family. My hand has been withered, I am powerless to love my wife as I ought; powerless to be as gentle as I should; powerless to show love to my children; and powerless to serve God as I am supposed to. Here I am Lord, withered hand and all. Here I am, just as I am."

Brethren, we will never be healed faking and frauding. Until we stand up as men, our families will hurt. Jesus said, "Stand up...." Jesus also said, "step forth!" "Come to the front!" "Quit hiding behind dress tails. Come from under those petticoats." A man can never lead from the rear, always in hiding. We should all be concerned about these brethren, who impregnate women and then run and hide. White folk should not have to come and take our money and give it to our children. Are we so powerless that white folk have to make us care for own? Even in the church, very few men come forth in Jesus' name.

The Lord wants to heal us, but we can never be healed hiding the fact that we feel so powerless. Jesus still calls us to, "Stand up!" He still calls us to, "Come forth." He also calls us to, "stretch out your hand."

I finally realize why Big Daddy had so much power. Big Daddy, whose father and grandfather were slaves, stood for the Lord. Big Daddy stepped forth on God's word. And when the Lord's presence and power was near, Big Daddy stretched out his hand.

There he stood before Almighty God, troubled by the cares of a mean world. The South had turned on him and he didn't fully understand the West. His family was looking up to him, expecting his guidance and strength. In the words of the songwriter, he stretched out his hands and said:

> Father, I stretch my hands to Thee
> No other help I know.
> If Thou withdraw Thyself from me,
> Oh, whither shall I go.

Jesus heard the cry of the man with the withered hand and his hand was restored. God gave him power. God gave him strength. God gave him power to be a man for his family. God gave him power to be a man for his people. God gave him power to be a man of the church, and a man for the church.

> To serve this present age,
> My calling to fulfill.
> May all my power do engage
> to do the Master's will.

CREATING STRATEGIES FOR HEALTHY LIVING:
The Hope of Health for African Americans

Text: *"Now there were four leprous men at the entrance of the gate; and they said to one another, "Why are we sitting here until we die? If we say, 'We will enter the city' the famine is in the city, and we shall die there. And if we sit here, we die also. Now therefore, come, let us surrender to the army of the Syrians. If they keep us alive, we shall live; and if they kill us, we shall but die." And they rose at twilight to go to the camp of the Syrians; and when they had come to the outskirts of the Syrian camp, to their surprise no one was there. For the Lord had caused the army of the Syrians to hear noise of chariots and the noise of horses—the noises of a great army; so they said to one another, "Look the king of Israel has hired against us the kings of the Hittites and the kings of the Egyptians to attack us!" Therefore they arose and fled at twilight, and left the camp intact— their tents, their horses, and their donkeys—and they fled for their lives. And when these lepers came to the outskirts of the camp, they went into one tent and ate and drank, and carried from it silver and gold and clothing,and went and hid them; then they came back and entered another tent, and carried some from there also, and went and hid it. Then they said to one another, "We are not doing what is right. This day is a day of good news, and we remain silent. If we wait until morning light, some punishment will come upon us. Now therefore, come, let us go and tell the King's household." (**2Kings 7:3-9**, New Kings James Version)*

During my graduate school days at Vanderbilt University, I had the privilege of working in the wonderful world of hospital administration. I was a total alien in the world of medical care, not because it was dominated by whites; but because the language used in the medical world was different from the world of theology. One set of words that I will never forget were the words "Morbidity and Mortality."

Morbidity and Mortality are big words in the medical world. Dr. Bradley, the Head Anesthesiologist of Vanderbilt Hospital, was always referring to Morbidity and Mortality. There exist entire committees and boards, and journalist reviews on "Morbidity and Mortality."

Morbidity refers to disease and mortality refers to death. Morbidity and Mortality refer to the patterns of disease rate and death rate. In the world of medicine a chief concern of all is the rate of disease and death. This concern with morbidity and mortality sparked my curiosity. Why should the people who are supposed to be busy keeping folk alive be so obsessed with the rate of disease and death? They ought to be curing diseases and slowing down death. Why all of this morbidity and mortality? The world of medicine keeps a close eye on disease and death because they want to know how well they are doing. Are there areas of disease where we are making progress? And, are there more/less people dying from certain diseases? In simpler terms, what are people dying from and how might the medical world responsibly respond?

This ought to interest us who have put so much weight in religion. We, who have had to depend heavily upon the church, ought to be interested in what people are dying from and how religion might responsibly respond. Contrary to the thinking of many, the church does not exist for the purpose of funerals. Preachers are not called just to give last rites and committals. The sanctuary is not to be perceived as some glorified casket, although it appears that way on many Sundays. Whether we accept it or not, we are a part of a faith that is concerned about life. Jesus said, "I come that they may have life." He identified Himself as "the way, the truth, and the life." Not even Jesus was satisfied with making the graveyard His life-goal. He rose and took the sting out of death and the victory out of the grave.

It does seem logical that good religion ought to lead to good health, and that good health is good religion. The church created hospitals, so that people could get well and serve God. Our ministry to the sick is fueled by the belief that God wants people well. Sickness, or bad health, is the result of sin. It is not the goal of the church. Therefore, I want to submit that the health of our people depends upon our creating strategies that enhance the health of African Americans.

If our faith is to really make a difference in people's lives, the Black church must become creatively involved in promoting health among Black people. We must look at the morbidity and mortality notes and determine what is killing our people and how fast are we dying from it. And, what can we do, as a religious body, to help keep people alive?

I do not approach this sermon easily. I wrestled with how to sermonize health to heaven-bound folk, who would rather pray than take medicine. The words of Paul caught my attention. **"Present your body as a living sacrifice, holy and acceptable to God which is your reasonable service." "You are the body of Christ...." "Your body is the temple of God."** Even Jesus' allusion to the sacraments as "this is my body" pointed to a concern of a healthy body. The church is Biblically pictured as "one body with many members." This message is important to us because we cannot even be a good body of Christ, if we, as members of the body, are always sick. Sick body parts affect the whole body and sick bodies are evidences of sick souls. Furthermore, freedom and equal rights are irrelevant to a people plagued by sickness and disease. "He who is not sick, needs not a physician." But, those who are free need to be well.

My sermonic struggle led me to a sick foursome hanging out at the gates of Samaria. The Bible describes these four men as being afflicted with the leprosy. Leprosy was a hideous disease that the early Jews did not know how to deal with. It was a noticeable sickness believed to be the punishment of God that resulted in slow death. Lepers were isolated from the mainstream of society and ordered not to subject others to their afflictions. Lepers were set apart from family, friends, and even the church. They lived a separate and lonely life that was legally and religiously imposed by the society.

Outside of the city of Samaria, I found four sick men living out their days as they had been instructed. The society had limited their interaction with people by giving them a place at the gate. They could look in but they could not go in. They were socially and systematically excluded. It was understood by all, accepted by the sick, sanctioned by the church, that the place of those with histories of sickness was outside of the city. Interestingly, a famine struck the city. However, an economic downturn disrupted the life of the city. The monies once stingily allocated to the leprosy fund dried up. The first to feel the economic crunch were those assigned as sick. This prompted this sick foursome into creative action. They decided they were going to do something creative about their sick situation, or die trying.

Maybe no one has heard about it, but African Americans have been assigned to the gate. I say we have been assigned to the gate because there is a connection between where we live and the morbidity and mortality rate. Honest professionals of medicine have confessed that there is a connection between racism and bad health. In their own words they say, "disease and illness are socially produced." Where you live and how you live has all to do with what's going to kill you. With all of the advances in medicine, Black folk are still prone to die more quickly from more diseases than white folk. We are still less likely to have access to affordable health care; we will know less about preventive health practices, and most likely will die before our white counterparts. The real test of a nation's strength is its infant mortality rate, that is, the rate in which children live past their first birthday. America is number one in military, but number nineteen in infant mortality. Why? Because Black babies are twice as likely to die before their first birthday than white babies. When Black teenage unemployment goes up and Black teenage pregnancy goes up, while social programs go down—the death of Black children is inevitable.

It is no accident that sickle-cell is a Black disease. It is no accident that AIDS will proportionately kill more blacks than whites. It is no accident that deaths by cancer are increasing in the Black community, but decreasing in the white community. It is no accident that the South is not only known as the "Black Belt"; but it is also known as the "stroke belt," because strokes are going up in the Black community. It is no accident that stress-related diseases afflict the Black community more than other communities. Certainly, there is nothing more stressful than having to be eternally subjected to racism. It is no accident that Blacks suffer from obesity and poor nutrition at the same time. We are overweight, but undernourished.

We have been assigned to the gate, where poor housing is standard. We have been assigned to the gate, where sanitary conditions do not exist. We have been assigned to the gate, where health insurance is too expensive for most. We have been assigned to the gate, where trash is dumped and toxic waste is pumped. We have been assigned to the gate, where drugs are used to escape the ugliness. We have been assigned to the gate and our health is getting worse and our pockets are getting emptier. It is time for us to begin creating strategies for healthy living.

I first preached this sermon to a group of Black doctors. I wanted to test my findings for relevancy. I also lifted before the doctors that I am concerned that most of what you all are doing is not healthcare, it is medical care. Doctors, Black and white, are having a profitable field day treating sick people, rather than helping people avoid sickness. It has become good business (as well as easy business) to prescribe medicine, rather than to help people change their lifestyles. The doctors got real quiet, but conceded that I was correct in my understanding.

Brothers and Sisters, I need to tell you, this morning, that all of these hospital services sprouting up around us are not in the business of healthy living. They are here to treat sick folk and to keep on treating sick folk. Sickness is big business in America, even when the sick come from the gate.

Again, sickness is the result of sin. Our failing health is the result of our being out of harmony with the Creator. Jesus healed sick people, but He also instructed them to sin no more. In other words, Jesus saw that true health would come from a creative change in lifestyle. How can we shape a vision of hope for the health of Black people? What creative strategies can we provide for healthy living?

Contrary to popular thought, sick folk can help sick folk. This sick foursome at the gate helps us with our dilemma. At the gate of their misfortune, they provide practical strategies for healthy living. The logic of the lepers discussion helps us to see that the first step toward healthy living is to recognize the seriousness of our situation. A dialogue with reality can do much in bringing us to deal with reality. The reality of our plight must be honestly faced.

I lifted up but a few facts about the health of African Americans. We are seriously sick. We are seriously at the gate. We are seriously at risk of total annihilation. Our situation is of such that we can ill-afford to ignore it by playing games with one another. We are dying at faster rates than other people, by more things than other people are dying from, and doing fewer right things about our situation. I know you are waiting to get to heaven, "where there is no sickness, nor any dying." But we don't need to rush heaven by being negligent down here. We are not as healthy as we ought to be and not as healthy as we could be.

Reality informs us that the way we deal with life determines much of our health. This means that we have no room in our body for envy, jealousy, worry, insecurities, guilt, and other bad feelings about self nor others. We cannot think bad thoughts and live healthy lives. Also, living in a racist society has enough problems without our adding to it some bad habits. We are presently doing a lot of things to rush ourselves to the grave. We can ill-afford to do business-as-usual, when our very lives are at stake. Let's be honest and face up to the seriousness of our situation, or we sit here and die.

The sick foursome further helps us because they recognized that good health ultimately demands a decision to live, even at the risk of death. They made a decision to do something radical so that they might live. If they stayed where they were, doing business as usual, they were sure to die. If they confronted the Syrians, the powers-that-be, they could get killed, or, they might live. They took a chance on doing something, rather than doing nothing. They decided to confront those who held the resources for life.

Black folk have historically been high on talk, but short on risk-taking resolve. We talk a good talk, but we do very little. I know the white folk have done much to instill fear within us. But if we are to ever have hope for healthy living, we will have to decide to confront the powers-that-be. Mrs. Clinton needs to be hearing from some sick folk, rather than powerful folk. She needs to be hearing from the people at the gate, rather than city keepers. It's risky business! But, we need a coalition of gate-people to crash the party in Washington and declare that we want to live.

Some creative gate-folk need to crash some of our church meetings and declare an end to business-as-usual. Some gate-people need to break in on Black Baptist church leadership and say, "We don't really care about who is on what board, or on this committee. We are not concerned about positions of power and process. The keeping of the temple is not that important. What is important is that we are sick, about to die, and we want to live. Do you have anything that's good for living? What are you doing for the health of all these little Black children, who are dying at the gate?" Jesus said, **"Inasmuch as you did it unto the least of these, you did it also unto me."**

The lepers entered the city and discovered that God had already taken care of business. The powers-that-be had been reduced to the powers-that-were. The-powers-that-be were less than the powers of God. Upon entering the city, the lepers had an experience with life that they never had before. They were able to walk where they wanted to walk. They lived like they had never lived before. I am certain that they felt better than they had ever felt. They were able to have whatever their hearts desired. They indulged themselves and enjoyed themselves. They lived wherever they wanted to live. However, the blessings of the moment awakened their sense of responsibility. They said to one another, **"We are not doing what is right. This day is a day of good tidings, and we remain silent. If we wait until the morning comes, some mischief will come upon us. Now therefore, come, let us go and tell the king's household."**

Brothers and Sisters, we need to recognize that the recovery of health calls for the sharing of health. When God blesses us, it is also a call to responsibility. If we don't share the good news with the king's people, some mischief will come upon us. One way of putting it is "Blessings indulged can become curses inflicted."

God has blessed the church with the good news of salvation. Salvation calls for loving **"the Lord God with your heart, and with all your soul, and with all your strength, and your neighbor as yourself."** I don't know about your understanding of salvation, but when God saved my soul—He made me whole. God healed my body. God rescued me from worry and delivered me from shame. God took me from drugs and riotous living. God freed me from cigarettes and bad eating habits. God gave me such health that "I looked at my hands and they looked new; I looked at my feet and they did, too." God gave me strength of limbs, alertness of mind, and clarity of speech.

If I don't tell the brothers at the gate, some mischief will come upon me. If I merely bless myself and stay in a church, some mischief will come upon me. So, I made up my mind to tell the gate-folk, " Today, is a day of good news."

> *Good news! A Savior has come.*
> *Good news! Healing is real.*
> *Good news! The weak have become strong.*
> *Good news! Death has no sting.*
> *Good news! Life is possible.*
> *Good news! The enemy has been conquered.*
> *Good news! The city has been opened.*
> *Good news! Health can be realized.*
> *Good news! Good news! Good news!*

IF THE CHILD HAD NOT CRIED

Text: *So Abraham rose early in the morning, and took bread and a skin of water, and putting it on her shoulder, he gave it and the boy to Hagar, and sent her away. Then she departed and wandered in the Wilderness of Beersheba. And the water in the skin was used up, and she placed the boy under one of the shrubs. Then she went and sat down across from him at a distance of about a bow-shot; for she said to herself, "Let me not see the death of the boy." So she sat opposite him, and lifted her voice and wept. And God heard the voice of the lad. Then the angel of God called to Hagar out of heaven, and said to her, "What ails you, Hagar? Fear not, for God has heard the voice of the lad where he is. "Arise, lift up the lad and hold him with your hand, for I will make him a great nation." And God opened her eyes, and she saw a well of water. Then she went and filled the skin with water, and gave the lad a drink. So God was with the lad; and he grew and dwelt in the wilderness, and became an archer. (Mark 21:14-20,* (New King James Version)

The Christmas season has come with such haste that I suspect many of us have had difficulty getting on board. Before we finished chewing the Thanksgiving turkey lights started flashing, commercials started jingling, trees went up inside of homes, nativity scenes were thrown on yards, and we were somehow supposed to automatically kick into the Christmas spirit. It appears that the merchants have been led to believe that all it takes to get us in the Christmas spirit is to put up some decorations and have a sale. Is this really what Christmas is all about?

When we consider Christmas, what really comes to our minds? My daughter asked me about eggnog. She wanted to know why I drink eggnog only during the Christmas season. "Is this the only time egg nog is sold?" she inquired. But really, my Brothers and Sisters, what honestly comes to our minds when we think of Christmas? Is it the increasingly extravagant lights that outline our homes, landscapes, and now even our cars? Is it the pine scent of trees that sprout up in our living rooms? Is it the expectation of gifts and giving? Does Christmas mean rich, starchy foods, washed down with eggnog, or other Christmas cheers? Does Christmas bring to us the warmness of family, friends, and even the sweet memories of dear ones past and gone? I know, for many, Christmas may mean a bumper to bumper excursion to some busy mall that has everything but what we want and very little of what we can afford. Indeed, Christmas has packed a lot of images and experiences into our minds.

Yet, as we consider Christmas, have we ever considered Christmas as being connected with a child who cried? A child whose parents were denied access to suitable lodging at His coming. A babe unexpectedly born in a stable. He cried. I could say beneath, but I must really say above— yes, above the extravagant commercialism of this market driven affair of our day is the humble, human reality of a child who cried. If He had not cried there would be no ornamented trees, fancy lights, Christmas carols, pine wreaths, and red ribbons. If He had not cried, there would be no Handel's Messiah, Singing Christmas trees, Nutcracker ballets, no poems to recite, no plays to perform, nor Baptist Candle Light services. If He had not cried, there would be no market to exploit; there would be no stockings to hang; there would be no Christmas to cheer; there would be no reason to swap gifts; and there would be no spirit of peace and goodwill toward all persons.

When I mused over the significance of the crying child, I was led to the incident of another crying child. Ishmael, which means "God will hear," preceded Jesus which means "God will save." Ishmael, the planned and determined son of Abraham, started life on the "wildside." He did not come into the world with a silver spoon in his mouth. He was not blessed with an abundance of resources as a child. He was not even privileged to live among those who were considered destined for promise. In fact, his arrival into the world was the result of human confusion and impatience. He was born into a situation where the adults of His world were confused about life's potential, as promised by God. Ishmael , along with his mother, was cast out with a welfare handout to wander in life's wilderness. Were it not for the boy, Ishmael, Hagar would have remained in servitude to the whims and wishes of Sarah. The boy, Ishmael, was the true catalyst for the restructuring of Hagar's world.

No one can change the structure of our lives like children. We can have our life mapped out to go in one direction, but let a child be born and our maps must be redesigned. Hagar had possibly envisioned her life to be forever in Sarah's camp, but Ishmael was born. A child came into her world and remade her whole world.

The coming of Ishmael disrupted not only Hagar's world, but it disrupted the world of Abraham and Sarah. Sarah, like so many of the privileged in life, lacked the creativity to include others in the promise. Sarah strongly contended that Ishmael would not be privy to the blessings of her son, so she arranged for Ishmael to be put out. Ishmael was cast out, excluded, expelled from privilege and promise. While in the wilderness, the water supply ran out. Hagar, in an act of desperation, placed Ishmael under a shrub. She distanced herself from the child, because she did not want to see him die. There away from the child, with a dried water bottle, no food, and worst of all no hope—she lifted her voice and cried.

As she wept in total despair, the Bible says, "God heard the voice of the lad." God heard the child's cry. On this commercially adulterated advent day, I want to propose that the cries of those who least deserve to suffer are heard by God. Ishmael did not ask to be born. He did not elect to be born the son of Abraham, nor half brother to Isaac. It was not Ishmael's fault that God waited before He blessed Sarah with a child. Ishmael was like so many Black children, who now suffer within the confusions of the adult world. Ishmael was like so many Black children who have been born in the wildernesses, and not privileged to economic promise.

Our children have been born in a world that will judge them by their skin color. They have been born with the painful scars of slavery blemishing their past. Our children have been born in a world that seems to have a conspiracy against Black dreamers. Our children have been born to parents, who are most confused about where we fit in the world. We are a tribe of Hagars, victims and victimizers. We transmit our fears and plug our children into our despair. Our children did not ask for all of this. They certainly do not deserve all of this. Maybe we don't hear their cries, but whether we hear or not—they are crying.

We hear the cries of children hip-hopping from sidewalk composed anthems. We hear the cries of our children in their rebellious dress codes, wearing big coats in the summer time and short pants in winter. We hear the cries of our children when they turn to drugs, hang out until morning with pals, party for nothing, have sex with anybody, chase fast cash, worship slick cars, and flirt with crime. Listen to the popular songs, the rage of some rappers, and view the worship of violence in most movies. Our children are crying out because the world, shaped by adults, has been terribly confused and tragically dishonest. It has been most confusing and we are so consumed with our selfish agendas that we don't even hear the children crying. We are just like Hagar. We are so far away from our children that we can't hear their cries.

Just this past week a United Nations contingency of armed soldiers, led by the United States, landed in Somalia. We have not gone public with inner frustrations. Black people, of sense and sensitivity, are deeply disturbed by this tragic chain of events. Someone ought to be asking, "Why is it that only black people are starving in Africa?" There are some white people living in Africa, but you never see them starving. Someone ought to be asking, "Why are there no Black people seen feeding the starving people in Somalia?" With all of the Black folk in the world, surely we are not so disorganized that we are powerless to help our own people. Someone ought truly to be asking, "What is the real agenda of these armed white folk in Somalia?" White folk surely don't love Black folk that much that they will interrupt their Christmas celebration to go to Africa to feed us.

I shared with a friend of mine that if Somalia was a nation of Black adults, no one would have heard their cry. The death cries of starving Black children proved irresistible to our sense of compassion. No one could justify allowing millions of Black people to die while we watch skinny little children, with protruding bellies and maggot-filled eyes, cry. If the children had not cried, believe me, millions of Black people would die and no one would know anything about it.

A cry is the most basic utterance of those who struggle for existence. The good news is God redemptively responds to those whose cries articulate a struggle for existence. The cries of children are primitive, "con"-free, undecorated, non-sugar-coated expressions of life's potential. That's why children cry! Children cry because life has potential. And since God is most concerned about life, God responds to the issues of life. A cry is about life.

The first thing that a child does when he/she is introduced into this world is to cry. Children do not come into the world dancing, rapping, or even eating. Children come crying. Furthermore, if the child does not cry, midwives/doctors will help the child cry. Cries are most heard when life is evident. The absence of a cry signals the absence of life. Cries are most heard when the basic necessities of life are unavoidable. You cannot avoid feeding, drying, caring, or resting a crying child. Cries are also most available when life is threatened.

A classmate recently shared with us a page out of his life. He said that some years ago he was awakened by the cry of his baby. As he made his way to the baby's bed to address the particular need of the child, he discovered that one-half of the house was on fire. If the child had not cried, the family would have been destroyed. The life of the family was severely threatened, but God heard the cry of the child.

Well, what is the current significance of the child's cry? How does the child's cry presently impact our lives? The story of Ishmael enriches our Christmas season, when we consider how the child's cry has blessed us. According to the Ishmael story, as well as the Christmas event, the child's cry helps us to see that God knows our situation. Ishmael, certainly undeserving of being cast into the wilderness, undeserving of politically constructed starvation, undeserving of inheriting parental confusion and despair, was known by God.

The list is long of the many things that the world wants us to believe that stack the deck against us. Yet, the One who made the world; the One, who created us; the One, who has made arrangements for us—He knows all about us. God knows our situation. God knows what we have and what we don't have. God knows where we have come from. God knows where we are going and God knows where we are.

The other day the newspaper reported about the discovery of a new monkey. While roaming the Rain Forests, scientists discovered a new species of monkey that had never been classified. The very fact that the scientists were out there in the Rain Forests looking indicates that they know that there remains the possibility of discovering new realities. The little monkeys were not lost. They had been there all the time. God has always known where the little monkeys were. Furthermore, if God knows where little monkeys are, He certainly knows where you and I are. Jesus informed us that God knows the number of hairs on our heads.

God is aware of the little mean things that have been done to keep us from being discovered as people of worth and wealth. God knows all about history. He knows that we have been troubled on every hand, pressed down, perplexed, forsaken, and struck down. The cry of the child helps us to see that the crying does not get God's attention; God is already giving attention to situation. God knows our situation, our circumstances, and our predicament.

Secondly, the child's cry helps us to see that God expects us to participate in the making of a people. God's message to Hagar, as called out by the angel, was **"Arise, lift up the lad and hold him with your hand, for I will make him a great nation."** "Called out" literally means to proclaim, "to preach." African Americans need to catch the true objective of preaching. Preaching is not about sensationalizing, emotionalizing, nor mere moralizing, To proclaim God's word has to do with building up a people. Brothers and Sisters, God wants us to get up, lift up, hold children in our hands as we make a great nation.

Our children are all we have that guarantee us that a nation can be made. We cannot afford to be cheap, lazy, non-committed, and distant with our children. We must put our all into our children, for our children represent our all. I cannot find anything more worthwhile for a church to be doing than investing in our children. Moreover, God expects us to participate in the making of a great nation. We cannot make a great nation being cheap, lazy, distant, apathetic, and non-committed. We must get up from our seats of self-pity and apathy and reach out and lift our children into greatness. God wants to do something with us that can only be done through us.

Thirdly, the child's cry helps us to see that God will reveal to us the necessary resources for our salvation. The Bible says, "And God opened her eyes, and she saw a well of water."A significant point must be made here. It was only after Hagar got up, lifted the child up, held him in her hand that God opened her eyes. Brothers and Sisters, God will only show us what we need when convinced that we will use it. God does not show us things that we are not ready to use. Hagar had committed herself to nation making, so God opened her eyes.

The Bible speaks of water, because water was so crucial to everything else. Without water, crops cannot grow, livestock cannot live, and human life is threatened. The Somalian tragedy is a tragedy of no water. Water is so critical to life that Jesus identified Himself as living water.

Black America may have some stuff that makes individuals look good, but what we need is what's critical to the life of the Black nation. One Black may get a $44 million baseball contract, but how do we explain teachers taking 12% cuts in salary? We need more people teaching than men swinging sticks at balls that have been wrapped in string, dipped in tar, and covered with leather. Teaching is nation building. Ball playing is ego building. The cry of the child helps us to see that God will provide what we need to do what we must do.

In verse 20, the story is summed up. Verse 20 says "And God was with the lad; and he grew and dwelt in the wilderness...." The cry of the child helps us to see that God is with us. The driving proposition of the Bible's witness is "God is with us." Even when Israel disobeyed God,

God sent prophets like Hosea who reminded Israel of one thing "God is with us." Hosea took a wife of whoredom. Gomer, who symbolized Israel, bore children. When Jezreel cried, Israel heard that God's judgment would be upon them. When Lo-ruhamah cried, Israel heard that God's mercy was with Judah. When Lo-Ammi cried, Israel heard "For you are not my people, and I will not be your God."

One thing that I want to assure my people of is that God is with us. I have three children, whose births were marked with cries. Their births also mark significant points in my faith journey. When Kamira cried, my life was filled with beautiful visions. In fact her name means " A Princess with a Beautiful Vision." Everything about my life was filled with the beautiful vision of God doing something wonderful with my life. If the child had not cried, I would have missed out on a wonderful vision of life. When Camau cried, my life was filling up with challenge. Camau's name means "A Quiet Warrior Who Sustains with Bravery." I had been pastor of the Olivet Church six months. My life needed the toughness of a warrior who could bravely endure. Being a pastor has called forth tremendous bravery. If the child had not cried, I would have never known how brave we could be. When Kamilah cried, my life was filled with struggle. I was struggling with everything. I was struggling with my ministry, the church, and even my marriage. Kamilah means "The Perfect Gift."

I never saw this before, until the other day. As many of you know Kamilah must live with a hearing challenge. She must live without 15% of her hearing. You may ask, "Reverend, how is a child with special challenges the perfect gift?" Kamilah cried into the world at a time in my life when I truly failed to listen to God. If the child had not cried, I would have never known how far I was drifting from the voice of God. If the child had not cried, my ministry would have become a stumbling block. If the child had not cried, I would have failed the pastorate. If the child had not cried, my family would have been destroyed. If the child had not cried, the vision would have shattered. Thank God, for the child's cry.

In Bethlehem, another child cried. If this child had not cried, we would all still be lost. If the child had not cried, salvation would be an illusion. If the child had not cried, love would be a delusion. If the child had not cried, sin's grip would destroy us. If the child had not cried, our guilt would cripple us. If the child had not cried, our burdens would have crushed us. If the child had not cried, our past would kill our future. I don't know about you, but I thank God for the child's cry. Since the child did cry, I can sing:

> *Joy to the world, The Lord has come*
> *Let earth receive her King.*
> *Let evr'y heart prepare Him room,*
> *And heaven and nature sing.*

Notes

Notes

Notes